Encou
M

D0427484

HENRI J.M. NOUWEN

Encounters with Merton

SPIRITUAL REFLECTIONS

A Crossroad Book
The Crossroad Publishing Company
New York

The Crossroad Publishing Company
16 Penn Plaza, 481 Eighth Avenue
New York, NY 10001

Copyright © 1972, 1981, by Henri J. M. Nouwen.

Previously published as *Pray to Live* (Fides, 1972) and *Thomas Merton: Contemplative Critic* (Harper & Row, San Francisco, 1981; Liguori/Triumph 1991).

A full list of acknowledgments appears on p. 135.

Printed in the United States of America

Cataloging-in-Publication Data is available from
the Library of Congress

ISBN 0-8245-2149-8

1 2 3 4 5 6 7 8 9 10   10 09 08 07 06 05 04

To Richard Alan White

Contents

Publisher's Note

This book, Henri Nouwen's reflections on the spirituality and life of Thomas Merton, was first written as *Bidden om het leven* (1970), soon appearing in English as *Pray to Live* (Fides, 1972; HarperSanFrancisco, 1981) and later as *Thomas Merton: Contemplative Critic* (Liguori Triumph, 1991). In those earlier editions, the book was divided into two halves — the first composed of Nouwen's commentary, the second containing sometimes extended excerpts from Merton's works, many of them hard to find or not yet published.

In preparation of the present edition for the Crossroad Nouwen Library, we integrated the two halves. Since Merton's works are now readily available, we removed or abridged the lengthier Merton excerpts, as well as those with cultural references requiring detailed explanation. For Nouwen's reflections, we did minor editing for style, gender inclusive language, and sociological terms, omitting nothing of the original content.

We are honored to have the opportunity to reintroduce this Nouwen classic to readers everywhere. Enjoy!

Preface to the Second Edition

By John Eudes Bamberger, O.C.S.O.
Abbot of the Genesee

As the second edition of this book goes to press, some twelve years have passed since the death of Thomas Merton in Bangkok. Many more of his own writings have become available to the public in recent times, and still more has been written about his life and his work. As the years pass, Merton continues to have a broad appeal to all types of men and women in varied life situations.

Recent writings about Merton reveal more sensitivity to his thought, especially to his prayer and monastic experience, than some of the publications that appeared shortly after his death. Yet much remains to be done before an adequate picture can capture the various shades, colors, and nuances of his responses to his times. It will be many more years before anything approaching a more definitive study of Merton can be written. Only a few of the fifteen journals he wrote are as

11

yet published; of the several thousand extant letters that contain some of his most personal thinking, only a very few have been made available. More important than either of these considerations, however, is that our times are still too near to those in which he wrote to evaluate and test the significance of many of his intuitions. A broader perspective is needed to fit into one picture the manifold themes and views that make up his life work and that express with adequate fullness the central realities that motivated and inspired him.

Still, Henri Nouwen has made broad and judicious use of the material available to him, and as a result he has been able to touch the heart of Thomas Merton's writings. There, in the heart, he has discovered the sources of Merton's inspiration and laid bare the connections between the various articulations of that vision of life and truth. He has seen that for Merton the way to relevance was the way of prayer and contemplation. Thomas Merton's social and political critique was based not on public debate and analysis but rather on a contemplative penetration into the heart of God, where he discovered the concrete person living on earth today. Merton himself brought all his own experience, his sins and sufferings, but also his sensitivity for beauty and truth, to this contemplative discovery. He came to feel the plight of all who know suffering, especially suffering inflicted by our fellow beings. And he felt it with passion of profound identification. No one more than Merton showed that the monastic life is not a retreat from reality. On the contrary, his social and political critique was the fruit of a compassion learned through a life of monastic ascesis and contemplation.

Henri Nouwen met Merton but once, yet by a sympathy of feeling and perception he has understood the central motivation force of Merton's life: meditation and prayer. He has seen this more truly and profoundly than some who, while claiming to be intimate friends of Merton, have altogether missed the point of his work and life through lack of feeling for his vision of God, humanity, and the cosmos. There is nothing surprising in this fact. True understanding depends not only on intelligence and proximity but above all on the heart.

Some of us had the chance to know Thomas Merton at Gethsemani for a long time, day by day, as monks know one another: simply, immediately, and unpretentiously. Some of us knew him too as a disciple knows a master, as a student knows a teacher, as a doctor knows a patient. We knew him in good days and bad, at his best and at his worst. We loved him as a brother, for he was a most lovable man in his unfailing and unpretentious accessibility. But above all we valued him as a man of God, with an unfailing and boundless enthusiasm for the monastic life and for the practices that were most central to contemplation, especially silence and solitude. We came to see that when he spoke with compassion for the oppressed of the earth, he spoke out of an awareness bought with his own anguish of heart and won by contemplative effort and insight.

We saw that he was compassionate because he knew himself as having received the compassion of God. And, finally, we saw that it was not so much his brilliant intelligence that gave him ready insight into sociological and political problems but rather his compassion.

Whatever may be said about Merton, if it will be said truly it must present his vision and his work as the fruit of the knowledge of God bought with a faith come alive through contemplation. Restoration of right order and peace in the world was for Merton the fruit of the vision of God arrived at through deep prayer. Henri Nouwen has seen Merton in this perspective, and this book clearly reveals some of the concrete, practical consequences of this way of experiencing life. In reading this book one can meet, for a brief moment, the living spirit of Merton. It is a refreshing encounter.

Abbreviations

Argument:	*My Argument with the Gestapo*
Conjectures:	*Conjectures of a Guilty Bystander*
Contemplation:	*Contemplation in a World of Action*
Faith:	*Faith and Violence*
Gandhi:	*Gandhi on Non-Violence*
Journal:	*The Secular Journal*
Mountain:	*The Seven Storey Mountain*
Seeds:	*Seeds of Destruction*
Sign:	*The Sign of Jonas*
Thoughts:	*Thoughts in Solitude*
Way:	*The Way of Chuang Tzu*
Zen:	*Zen and the Birds of Appetite*

Encounters with
Merton

Introduction

This book is an introduction to the life and thought of Thomas Merton. I met him only once, at the Abbey of Our Lady of Gethsemani in Kentucky. Yet thereafter, his person and work had such an impact on me that his sudden death stirred me as if it had been the death of one of my closest friends. It therefore seems natural for me to write for others about the man who has inspired me most in recent years.

I have tried here to uncover a few main trends in Merton's richly diverse and very productive life, in order to help people better understand his commitment to a contemplative critique of himself and his world. I hope that these short chapters will lead to an attentive meditation on Merton's own writings and to a continuing search for a contemplative foundation of our fragmented, restless lives....

I am very grateful to David Schlaver, Joe Freeman, Steve Thomas, and Barbara Henry for their generous help in the preparation of the manuscript, and to Inday Day for her competent secretarial assistance.

Special thanks I owe to John Eudes Bamberger, abbot of the Genesee, who for many years shared Merton's life as a monk at

Gethsemani Abbey in Kentucky and knew him well not only as his personal friend but also as his physician. His willingness to annotate the text made me overcome my hesitation to publish this book.

I have dedicated this book to Richard Alan White. His strong friendship and penetrating criticisms of my ideas and lifestyle gave me a deeper appreciation of Merton's intuition, that contemplation and revolution are two forms of radicalism that never should be separated.

A Short Biography

Thomas Merton was born on January 31, 1915, in Prades, France. His father was a painter, a New Zealander by birth; his mother, who also painted, originally came from Ohio. He was the older of two boys. (John Paul, born in 1918, was killed in 1943 during an air battle over the English Channel.) Although Thomas's father seldom or never visited a church, and his mother only now and then went to Quaker meetings, he was still baptized. This apparently had little impact on his upbringing.

In 1916 the Merton family moved to the United States and went to live on Long Island, New York. When Thomas was six his mother died, and he and his brother went to live with their grandparents, while his father, as before, continued to make trips to exhibit his canvases. In 1925 the elder Merton took his son with him to France and sent him to study in the lyceum in Montauban. In his fourteenth year Thomas went with his father to England and there entered high school in Oakham (Rutland). Already during this period he was developing a great interest in English literature;

William Blake, D. H. Lawrence, and James Joyce were his favorite authors.

In 1931, Thomas's father died in London from a brain tumor. Thomas, then sixteen, finished his studies in Oakham and received a scholarship for Clare College at Cambridge University, where he stayed until 1934. His summers he spent with his grandparents in the United States or traveling through Europe. During his trips in Italy and Germany, he gathered the impressions that he used in his first novel. In February 1935, at the age of twenty, he went to Columbia University and studied Spanish, German, geology, constitutional law, and French literature. There he joined the communist youth movement and became art editor for the student publication *Jester*.

Through the book *The Spirit of Medieval Philosophy* by Etienne Gilson, Thomas Merton became interested in scholasticism. He followed the courses on St. Thomas and Duns Scotus given by Daniel Walsh, who later became a friend of his. In these years he also developed a close friendship with Bramachari, a Buddhist monk who pointed him toward the great riches of Christendom. In 1938 he undertook religion lessons with Father Moore, who received him into the Catholic Church on November 16 of that year.

At twenty-four, upon receiving his master's degree in English literature at Columbia, he became an English teacher at Columbia University Extension, New York, and a book reviewer for the *New York Times* and the *New York Herald Tribune*. Through many conversations with his friend Bob Lax and by studying St. John of the Cross, he began to feel a desire to become a priest.

At first he wanted to become a Franciscan, but when it was made clear to him in a discourteous manner that he didn't have a vocation, he dropped this plan.

From 1939 to 1941 he taught English at St. Bonaventure's College in Olean, New York. During his two years there, Thomas Merton led an almost monastic life, wrote a diary and three novels — none of which was accepted for publication — and went on retreat at the Trappist monastery in Gethsemani, Kentucky. In 1941 Merton left St. Bonaventure's and went to work in the African American ghetto of Harlem under the direction of Baroness Catherine de Hueck.

After a second visit to the Trappists of Gethsemani, he decided to join them. He gave his clothes to the African Americans in Harlem and his books to the Franciscans and a friend. He tore up two of his novels and sent the rest of his work — his poetry, a manuscript of the novel *Journal of My Escape from the Nazis,* and his diary — to his friend Mark Van Doren.

Completely alone, with a small duffel bag in his hand, twenty-six-year-old Thomas Merton arrived at Gethsemani on December 10, 1942. There he lived as a member of the community until 1968, the last three years in a hermitage.

The publication of his autobiography, *The Seven Storey Mountain,* in 1948 suddenly made Merton an internationally known author, whose many books and articles deepened the spiritual life of many Christians and non-Christians throughout the world. In the twenty-six years of his Trappist life he left the cloister on only a few occasions. When he was fifty-three, in 1968, he received permission to make an orientation trip to the Far East. In attending this conference of abbots from Christian contemplative monasteries in Asia, he had hoped to become more intimate with Eastern spirituality. He visited many Buddhist monasteries, spoke on various occasions with the Dalai Lama, led discussions, and gave a lecture for the monks and nuns who had gathered for the conference.

On December 10, 1968, shortly after his lecture, he was found dead in his room. Contact with a defectively wired fan had electrocuted him. His body was brought back to his monastery, and on December 17 he was buried at Gethsemani.

Chapter One

From Sarcasm to Contemplation

Today we know Thomas Merton as one of the most impressive contemplatives of our time. Yet in his youth, we find him more a sardonic and witty spectator, in whom the seeds of contemplation only gradually come to fruition. Even more than his detailed autobiography, *The Seven Storey Mountain*, which Thomas Merton wrote in Gethsemani, his diary *The Secular Journal* unveils for us the life of the young Merton. In this diary, written long before it was published, we find the direct, spontaneous reactions of a young intellectual who does not yet know whether the world is to be loved or ridiculed.

The short, fragmentary diary lets us see Thomas Merton as an intelligent, well-read, and well-traveled "graduate," who with poignant sarcasm perceives his surroundings and gives his commentary on them. Most noticeable in the *Journal*, perhaps, is the somewhat brutal nonchalance with which he criticizes the "stage" of the world. Nevertheless, by reading it we quickly recognize its writer to be an exceptionally sensitive young man, one who, parentless since his sixteenth year, was constantly searching, through travel and books, for something or someone to whom he could give his full dedication.

Distant Perception

When Merton, almost twenty years after writing this diary, prepared the foreword for its publication, he said:

> Certainly the views and aspirations expressed, at times, with such dogmatic severity, have come to be softened and tempered with the passage of time and with a more intimate contact with the spiritual problems of other people. I hope I may be forgiven for having allowed some of my youthful sarcasms to survive in these pages.
>
> (*Journal*, 8)

It is perhaps good that he did not scrap this sarcasm, because it gives us possibly the best introduction to his contemplative spirit. We find a delightful example of Merton's view of his surroundings in his ironic description of the reaction of museum visitors to a painting by Breughel. He writes:

> But what were the people saying about this picture? *Two girls, art students probably:* "It looks like one of the early French Impressionists." *One Killer-of-a-Fellow, with a mob*

of female admirers: "Excellent reporting: look at those knees." (The knees were very knobby.)

One of two girls (giggling): "Look at them kissing, there."

A man: "That one's drunk, I guess."

Another Killer: "You can tell it's a Dutch painting: not a skinny one in the whole bunch."

A man (foreign accent): "Country dance!"

A woman: "Look at those white aprons."

A man: "Some paunch!"

A man: "Look at the pipers."

There were a lot of people who just read off the name, "Broo-gul," and walked on unabashed. But at least they must have thought it important. They came across with the usual reaction of people who don't know pictures are there to be enjoyed, but think they are things that have to be learned by heart to impress the bourgeoisie: so they tried to remember the name. (*Journal,* 29)

That is the young Merton. With a distant grin he observes his fellow men and women around him. Sarcasm gets the better of him.

But this early sarcasm is certainly not implacable cynicism, for it can quite easily turn into violent indignation. In the room with the painting of El Greco he heard a woman say, "They're all dying of TB," and he wrote:

Of course there were plenty of comments on the misery and unhappiness of the age the painter lived in. What would be the good of turning around and asking the old lady: "If the world was dying then, what do you suppose it is doing now, in this age of hypochondriacs and murderers and sterilizers? How about *our* pictures, are they dying of anything? Or can they be said to die, when they can't even come to life in order to do so?" (*Journal*, 30)

Merton wrote this when he was twenty-three. Five years later he was a Trappist, and today he is rightly described as one of the most important spiritual writers of the twentieth century. It is surely true that the distant perception that appears in this diary has two sides. Distant perception leads to razor-sharp observation, which can lead to cynicism and bitterness; but it also can give rise to generous contemplation, which is the source of real care and human concern.

Merton had not yet experienced conversion and purification. But in the progress recorded in this diary, we see a deep earnestness, which in the beginning is still somewhat hidden, come more and more to the foreground. The first pages are filled mostly with critical commentary on the books that he had read, the paintings that he had seen, and the philosophies that inspired him. The gospel serves more to preserve all this at a certain playful distance than to let him feel deeply involved in his world. He wrote on William Blake, Dante, James

Joyce, and Graham Greene, on Fra Angelico, Breughel and El Greco, on St. Thomas and St. Augustine with a pointedness but also with the somewhat free-wheeling ease of a snobbish student. Scarcely two years a Catholic, he observed the world through the eyes of an enthusiastic but still naive convert.

Thus he traveled to Cuba, where he glorified in rich poetical terms the life of Havana and made a fiery plea for the genuineness of the Spanish religiosity in contrast to the superficiality of American thought. His Cuban diary perhaps belongs with the best prose he ever wrote.

Choices

Back in New York, his journal tells us he busied himself again with writers, painters, and philosophers, until on April 7, 1941, on a trip to Gethsemani he wrote: "I should tear out all the other pages of this book, and all the other pages of anything else I have ever written and begin here" (*Journal*, 155). That sounds like the cry of a man who suddenly sees himself and his world in their true form. As if unmasking his ironic distance and discovering it to be vanity, he wrote:

I wonder if I have learned enough to pray for humility. I desire only one thing: to love God. Those who love Him, keep His commandments. I only desire to do one thing: to follow his will. I pray that I am at least beginning to

know what that may mean. Could it ever possibly mean
that I might some day become a monk in this monastery?
(*Journal*, 172)

The impact of this new experience was profound. Back in
New York he seemed to have lost orientation. He mocked his
interest in literature:

I am amazed at all the novels I read between the ages
of seventeen and twenty. I was never able to swal-
low Hardy, although I read practically everything else,
D. H. Lawrence, Stella Benson, Virginia Woolf, John Dos
Passos, Jules Romains, Hemingway, Balzac, Flaubert,
Celine, even some short stories by Stefan Zweig, some
Vicki Baum, and the other day when I was sitting in the
sun I remembered with embarrassment how I tried to
explain to my godfather why I liked Luciano Zuccoli's
bad pornographic novel *La Divina Fanciulla.* I said it was
"very Italian." I have read enough novels, and I don't
want to read any more. Also, I think the novel is a lousy
art form anyway. (*Journal*, 183)

The people around him became riddles to him. He didn't
speak of them anymore with a mocking smile, but in despairing ignorance. "I have never been more convinced than now
that I see absolutely no sense in what people do" (*Journal*,
16). His novel *My Argument with the Gestapo,* which he wrote

The more we love earthly things,
reputation, importance, ease,
success and pleasures, for ourselves,
the less we love God.
—Merton

Detachment in poverty
offers the unheard-of chance
to stand without fear
in a violent world.
—Nouwen

in the summer of 1941 after his visit to the Trappists, is like a long litany, with the refrain: I can't understand them: the soldiers who fight, the sailors who drown, the Germans who attack, the English who defend, the people who busy themselves, I cannot understand them. What is the sense in what people do? (see *Argument*, 55–56).

In between he worked and lived at St. Bonaventure's College but constantly questioned whether this kind of teaching was the way he wanted to follow Christ. He felt the contradiction between the rich St. Patrick's Cathedral on Fifth Avenue and the poor black children of Harlem. He went to Harlem to work, but distrusted his motives. Wasn't this a compromise? Wasn't something more being demanded of him? Harlem or the Trappists? The choice preoccupied him, but it didn't make him anxious. He laughed at his busy past and wrote:

No need for anything new, or for any excitement whatever. If I pray, either I will change my mind or I will not [about going to work in Harlem]. In any case, God will guide me. No need to be up in arms, no need to be anything other than what I am — but I will pray and fast hard. No more excitements, arguments, tearing of hair, trips to Cuba and grandiose "farewell world" gestures. No need for anything special — special joy or special sorrow, special excitement or special torment. Everything is indifferent except prayer, fasting, meditation and work. (*Journal*, 216)

Still, his work in Harlem did not keep his thoughts about Gethsemani from haunting him. On November 27, 1941, he wrote: "Why doesn't this idea of the Trappists leave me?" He answered his own question: "Perhaps I cling to my independence, to the chance to write, to go where I like in the world." Finally he writes:

> But going to the Trappists is exciting, it fills me with awe and desire. I return to the idea again and again: "Give up *everything!*" (*Journal*, 222–23)

With these words *The Secular Journal* closes, and with them, the life of the young Merton. Two weeks later he reported to Gethsemani to begin a spiritual journey, one whose intensity and fascination make the many other journeys described in *The Seven Storey Mountain* seem like child's play.

FOR MEDITATION

On God's nature

It is said that while the Germans were desecrating a church somewhere in Poland, some German sergeant, cockeyed with the excitement, stood up in front of the altar and yelled out that if there was a God He would want to prove His existence at once by striking down such a bold and important and terrifying fellow as this sergeant. God did not strike him down. The sergeant went away still excited, and probably the unhappiest man in the world: God had not acted like a Nazi. God was not, in fact, a Nazi, and God's justice (which everybody obscurely knows about in his bones, no matter what he tries to say he thinks) is inexpressibly different from the petty bloodthirsty revenge of Nazis. (May 21, 1940, *Journal*, 99)

On popular opinion

In this situation, where there are hundreds of people with no real faith, who don't really believe anything much, long inquiries are constantly being carried out as to what various persons "believe." Scientists, advertising men, sociologists, soldiers, critics, are all asked what they believe inasmuch as they are scientists, advertising men, etc. Apparently there is a separate belief appropriate to every walk of life. Anyway, they all answer with brisk one-thousand-word articles stating some opinion or other that they have picked up somewhere. The result is enough to make you break down and sob.

(May 30, 1940, *Journal*, 116–17)

On the reasons for peace

We have no peace because we have done nothing to keep peace, not even prayed for it! We have not even *desired* peace except for the wrong reasons: because we didn't want to get hurt, we didn't want to suffer. But if the best reason we have for desiring peace is only that we are cowards, then we are lost from the start, because the enemy only sees in our cowardice his first and most effective weapon.

(June 25, 1940, *Journal*, 121–22)

On our guilt

When I pray for peace I pray for the following miracle. That God move all men to pray and do penance and recognize each one his own great guilt, because we are all guilty of this war, in a way. [Leon] Bloy says somewhere, of a murderer, that all the people were a tree of which this murderer was only one of the fruits, and that applies to Hitler: We are a tree, of which he is one of the fruits, and we all nourish him, and he thrives most of all on our hatred and condemnation of him, when that condemnation disregards our own guilt, and piles the responsibility for everything upon somebody else's sins!

(February 22, 1941, *Journal*, 164–65)

On the religious life

The religious life exists and thrives not in buildings or dead things or flowers or beasts but in the soul. And there it exists not as a "good feeling" but as a constant purpose, an unending love that expresses itself now as patience, now as humility, now as courage, now as self-denial, now as justice, but always in a strong knot of faith and hope, and all of these are nothing but aspects of one constant deep desire, charity, love.

(April 8, 1941, *Journal,* 190)

On nothingness

We must long to learn the secret of our own nothingness (not God's secret first of all, but our own secret). But God alone can show us our own secret. Once we see it, we can seek to receive His love into our hearts, and we can desire to become like Him. Indeed, by His love we can begin to become like ourselves — that is, we can find our own true selves, for we are made in His image and likeness.

(April 10, 1941, *Journal,* 197)

On annihilation

The measure of our identity, or our being (for here the two mean exactly the same thing) is the amount of our love for God. The more we love earthly things, reputation, importance, ease, success and pleasures, for ourselves, the less we love God. Our identity gets dissipated among a lot of things that do not have the value we imagine we see in them, and we are lost in them: we know it obscurely by the way all these things disappoint us and sicken us once we get what we have desired. Yet we still bring ourselves to nothing, annihilate our lives by trying to fulfill them on things that are incapable of doing so. When we really come to die, at last, we suddenly know how much we have squandered and thrown away, and we see that we are truly annihilated by our own sick desires: we were nothing, but everything God gave us we have also reduced to nothing, and now we are pure death.

(September 3, 1941, Journal, 243–44)

Chapter Two

The Way to Silence

Once inside the walls of the Trappist abbey in Kentucky, Merton undertook a difficult path. Yet besides what we have discussed in the first chapter, there were various signs that brought him there. These were books, people, and events — all of which made an impression on a young man, born of very artistic parents, already many years an orphan, constantly traveling between France, England, and the United States. It is not surprising that we are dealing here with a man who was a searching person. He sought a place where he could feel at home, he sought an insight by which to bring order to the endless series of opposing ideas that poured over him in his various schools, and he sought after beauty that could give him the satisfaction he had fleetingly found in the many things that were presented to him as art.

The influence of the books, people, and events that brought Thomas Merton to Gethsemani can be understood only if we keep in mind his intense personality, which registered with a maximum sensitivity everything that he read, saw, and experienced, always posing the question as large as life itself: "What can I say 'yes' to, without reserve?"

Books

When Thomas Merton entered Columbia University in 1935, he was already very well read. In the London milieu, to which his godfather had introduced him, Ernest Hemingway, James Joyce, D. H. Lawrence, Evelyn Waugh, and Celine had become very familiar names to him. But there are two books especially that brought him to a deeper level of knowledge than the London literary circle: *The Spirit of Medieval Philosophy* by Etienne Gilson and *Ends and Means* by Aldous Huxley.

With a sense of humor, Merton told how thankful he was that he hadn't thrown Gilson's book out the train window when he discovered to his great surprise the "Nihil obstat — imprimatur" and became conscious, to the point of aversion, that it was a Roman Catholic book.

From Gilson, Merton learned of the concept *aseitas*. Merton wrote:

In this one word, which can be applied to God alone, and which expresses His most characteristic attribute, I discovered an entirely new concept of God — a concept which showed me at once that the belief of Catholics was by no means the vague and rather superstitious hangover from an unscientific age that I had believed it to be. On the contrary, here was a notion of God that was at the same time deep, precise, simple and accurate and, what is more, charged with implications which I could not even begin to appreciate, but which I could at least dimly estimate, even with my own lack of philosophical training. (*Mountain,* 172)

Aldous Huxley, who was one of Merton's favorite novelists through his book *Ends and Means,* was the first to bring him into contact with mysticism. Merton says about Huxley:

He had read widely and deeply and intelligently in all kinds of Christian and Oriental mystical literature, and had come out with the astonishing truth that all this, far from being a mixture of dreams and magic and charlatanism, was very real and very serious.

(*Mountain,* 185)

To his alarm, Merton read the conclusion of Huxley, that, if we want to live differently from wild beasts, we must free the spirit by means of prayer and asceticism. The word "asceticism" had up to now only meant a twisting of nature, but Huxley showed him that it is only through asceticism that the spirit can become itself and find God. Merton shrank from this, but still began hesitatingly to feel out this way.

My first human act
is the recognition of how much
I owe everybody else.
—Merton

People who pray
stand receptive before the world.
They no longer grab but caress,
they no longer bite but kiss,
they no longer examine but admire.
—Nouwen

He bought the first volume of the works of John of the Cross, but actually had no idea where to begin. He wrote:

These words I underlined, although they amazed and dazzled me with their import, were all too simple for me to understand. They were too naked, too stripped of all duplicity and compromise for my complexity, perverted by many appetites. (*Mountain*, 238–39)

Nevertheless, he went on and as soon as he imposed upon himself a strongly ascetical lifestyle at St. Bonaventure's College, he began to understand even more that "dark night" of the Spanish mystic. At that time, for Merton, saints were still figures who live in bare and impoverished circumstances. In St. Therese of Lisieux he discovered that in the normal civil society, the requirements for sainthood and contemplation were also present. He wrote about her:

The one thing that seemed to me more or less impossible was for grace to penetrate the thick, resilient hide of bourgeois smugness and really take hold of the immortal soul beneath that surface, in order to make something out of it. At best, I thought, such people might turn out to be harmless prigs: but great sanctity? Never! ... However, no sooner had I got a faint glimpse of the real character and the real spirituality of St. Therese, than I was immediately and strongly attracted to her — an attraction that was the work of grace, since, as I say, it took me, in one jump, clean through a thousand psychological obstacles and repugnances. (*Mountain*, 354)

If it was especially John of the Cross and Therese of Lisieux who brought him in closer contact with Christian mysticism, it was Ignatius of Loyola who brought him to prayer. The *Spiritual Exercises* had been standing in his bookcase for a long time, but he was a little bit afraid of them, because of "having somewhere acquired a false impression that if you did not look out they would plunge you head-first into mysticism before you were aware of it" (*Mountain*, 268). Still he wanted to try it, and set up his own discipline. He wrote in his autobiography:

As far as I remember, I devoted a whole month to the *Exercises*, taking one hour each day. I took a quiet hour, in the afternoon, in my room on Perry Street: and since I now lived in the back of the house, there were no street noises to worry me. It was really quite silent. With the windows closed, since it was winter, I could not even hear any of the neighborhood's five thousand radios.

The book said the room should be darkened, and I pulled down the blinds so that there was just enough light left for me to see the pages, and to look at the Crucifix on the wall over my bed. And the book also invited me to consider what kind of a position I should take for my meditation. It left me plenty of freedom of choice, so long as I remained more or less the way I was, once I had settled down, and did not go promenading around the room scratching my head and talking to myself.

So I thought and prayed awhile over this momentous problem, and finally decided to make my meditations sitting cross-legged on the floor. I think the Jesuits would have had a nasty shock if they had walked in and seen me doing their *Spiritual Exercises* sitting there like Mahatma Gandhi. But it worked very well. Most of the time I kept my eyes on the Crucifix or on the floor, when I did not have to look at the book.

And so, having prayed, sitting on the floor, I began to consider the reason why God had brought me into the world. (*Mountain*, 268–69)

This increasing ease with prayer had a deep effect on the lifestyle of Thomas Merton. Most noticeable was his almost obvious longing for a more disciplined lifestyle and his growing openness for the beauties of nature. In the beginning his new "rule" was the most visible result. This seemed to come forth almost spontaneously out of his prayer life. He wrote:

I found that, almost without realizing it, I had little by little reorganized the pattern of my life on a stricter plan, getting up earlier in the morning, saying the Little Hours about dawn, or before it when the days got shorter, as a preparation for Mass and Communion. Now, too, I took three quarters of an hour in the morning for mental prayer. I was doing a lot of spiritual reading.

(*Mountain*, 352)

It seemed as if the spiritual freedom that Merton increasingly acquired also made him more open-minded and free in respect to his environment. He was less tense, less agitated, less needy, less restless, and the nature in which he lived — which up to then he had hardly noticed — opened up for him into a beauty that he had never before seen.

It is impressive to see how prayer opens one's eyes to nature. Prayer makes people contemplative and attentive. In place of manipulating, people who pray stand receptive before the world. They no longer grab but caress, they no longer bite but kiss, they no longer examine but admire. To prayerful people, nature can show itself completely renewed. Instead of an obstacle, it becomes a way; instead of an invulnerable shield, it becomes a veil that gives a preview of unknown horizons.

At first Thomas Merton was still too busy with his own inner life to be able to stand completely open to nature. Moreover, how could he experience nature in the city? But whenever he was with his friends in a summer cottage, nature began to speak a language he never found in books, and his eyes wandered from the words to the trees. He wrote:

It was a cool summer evening. As I was sitting in the driveway...with the book in my lap I looked down at the lights of the cars crawling up the road from the valley. I looked at the dark outline of the wooded hills and at the stars that were coming out in the eastern sky. The words of the Vulgate text rang and echoed in my heart: *"Qui facit Arcturum et Oriona..."*; "Who makest Arcturus and Orion and Hyades and the inner parts of the South...." (*Mountain*, 293)

Still these experiences of nature remained exceptional. Books still held his preference. Only later, at the abbey, after living for many years in the Kentucky hills did an intimacy with nature nourish his prayer constantly.

People

Next to books, it was especially people who led Merton to Gethsemani. Despite the fact that *The Secular Journal* and *The Seven Storey Mountain* are full of names of people Thomas Merton had known in his youth, only a few stand out as really influential figures. Four names are worthy of our attention: Mark Van Doren, Daniel Walsh, Bramachari, and Bob Lax.

Mark Van Doren and Daniel Walsh were both teachers at Columbia. Through their personality and manner of teaching, they created some order in the abundance of ideas and feelings of the young Merton. Remarkably, he got to know the two teachers only by chance, and he enrolled in their courses though they were unnecessary for his course of study.

If there was anyone through whom Merton was inspired, it was certainly Mark Van Doren. It is fascinating to read how Merton described this man who was his teacher in many respects. Merton wrote about Van Doren's lectures in English literature:

> It was the best course I ever had at college. And it did me the most good, in many different ways. It was the only place where I ever heard anything really sensible said about any of the things that were really fundamental: life, death, time, love, sorrow, fear, wisdom, suffering, eternity. . . . Mark's balanced and sensitive and clear way of seeing things, at once simple and yet capable of subtlety, being fundamentally scholastic, though not necessarily and explicitly Christian, presented these things in ways that made them live within us, and with a life that was healthy and permanent and productive. This class was one of the few things that could persuade me to get on the train and go to Columbia at all.
>
> (*Mountain*, 180)

In Merton's description of Van Doren's teaching method, his picture of the ideal teacher comes out. He said:

Do not think that Mark was simply priming his students with thoughts of his own, and then making the thought stick to their minds by getting them to give it back to him as their own. Far from it. What he did have was the gift of communicating to them something of his own vital interest in things, something of his manner of approach: but the results were sometimes quite unexpected — and by that I mean good in a way that he had not anticipated, casting lights that he had not himself foreseen.

Now a man who can go for year after year ... without having any time to waste in flattering and cajoling his students with any kind of a fancy act, or with jokes, or with storms of temperament, or periodic tirades — whole classes spent in threats and imprecations, to disguise the fact that the professor himself has come in unprepared — one who can do without all these nonessentials both honors his vocation and makes it fruitful. (*Mountain*, 139–40)

Daniel Walsh is the second figure at Columbia who meant a lot to Merton. Unlike Mark Van Doren, he was a guest lecturer on Thomas Aquinas at Columbia. He too was described by Merton as an exceptional teacher. Walsh, he wrote:

had nothing of the supercilious self-assurance of the ordinary professor: he did not need this frail and artificial armor for his own insufficiency. He did not need to hide behind tricks and vanities any more than Mark Van Doren did; he never even needed to be brilliant. In his smiling simplicity he used to efface himself entirely in the solid and powerful mind of St. Thomas.

(*Mountain*, 219)

Even before Merton began to attend the lectures of Walsh, he has visited him and presented him with his idea of becoming a priest. Together they talked about all the different orders and eventually settled on the Franciscans as the best type for Merton. But then Walsh told him enthusiastically about Gethsemani and urged him to go there on retreat.

Years later, long after Merton became a Trappist, Walsh came to Gethsemani to teach philosophy, and in 1967 he himself was ordained a priest in the diocese of Louisville.

Both Mark Van Doren and Daniel Walsh were people who radiated a great inner calm. They were not influenced very much by university customs; they were very simple and clear in their lectures, were direct and personal in their dealings with students, and were prepared through their vision and personality to create a unity in the thoughts and feelings of the young Merton. Both intellectually and emotionally he found a home with them, and he came in contact with a deeper current that was hidden under the surface of a restless student life.

A completely different figure who left a deep influence on Thomas Merton was the Indian monk referred to as Dr. Bramachari (which is the Hindu term for monk). Merton wrote about him with much humor, great respect, and deep reverence. After he met Bramachari for the first time at Grand Central Station in New York, he wrote:

There stood a shy little man, very happy, with a huge smile, all teeth, in the midst of his brown face. And on the top of his head was a yellow turban with Hindu prayers written all over it in red. And, on his feet, sure enough: sneakers. (*Mountain*, 195)

Merton and Bramachari became friends. Merton admired the sympathetic way in which Bramachari criticized the Western world and relativized everything that people in the university world found so important:

He was never sarcastic, never ironical or unkind in his criticisms: in fact he did not make many judgments at all, especially adverse ones. He would simply make statements of fact, and then burst out laughing — his laughter was quiet and ingenuous, and it expressed his complete amazement at the very possibility that people should live the way he saw them living all around him.

(*Mountain*, 196)

Bramachari did not at all try to give Merton an insight into his own belief, let alone to force any convictions on him. On the contrary, he was the one who said to Merton: "There are many beautiful mystical books written by the Christians. You should read St. Augustine's *Confessions,* and *The Imitation of Christ*" (*Mountain,* 198).

This was at the very time that Merton was wrestling through the French translation of hundreds of strange Eastern texts. He found them very mysterious and complicated, and in the long run they didn't interest him. Thus he was all the more impressed when this Hindu monk pointed him to the Christian mystical tradition. Later he wrote:

> Now that I look back on those days, it seems to me very probable that one of the reasons why God had brought him all the way from India, was that he might say just that. (*Mountain,* 198)

It seems providential indeed that this Hindu monk relativized Merton's youthful curiosity for the East and made him sensitive to the richness of Western mysticism. Only after he had made this tradition his own would he be prepared for a real dialogue. But it would still be many years before Merton would meet Daisetz [D. T.] Suzuki, a man whom he judged to be of the same stature as Mahatma Gandhi and Albert Einstein, and one who stimulated and enriched his interest in the East. After his contact with Bramachari, the East disappeared from Merton's range of vision, and only after many years of absorption in his own tradition would it reappear on his horizon.

Of all the people who played a role in Merton's journey to Gethsemani, Bob Lax is certainly the most fascinating and perhaps also the central figure. The name of Bob Lax appears most often in *The Seven Storey Mountain,* and this remarkable figure emerges time and again at critical moments. He was not a teacher, like Van Doren and Walsh, nor was he as interesting an outsider as Bramachari. He belonged to the small circle of friends with whom Merton spent his student years in New York. Robert Gerdy, Seymour Freedgood, Edward Rice, Robert Lax, and Merton formed an artistic student club, of which Lax fascinated Merton the most. He was an intimate friend, indeed, but described with so much admiration and sympathy that it is clear how Merton constantly fell under the spell of this mysterious personality.

Remarkable, too, is the fact that Van Doren, Walsh, and Bramachari also came to Merton's attention through Lax, and that Merton continually reveals how much weight Lax's judgments carried for him.

Merton saw Lax for the first time sitting in the midst of a group of editors of the student magazine *Jester.* He wrote:

Taller than them all, and more serious, with a long face, like a horse, and a great mane of black hair on top of it, Bob Lax meditated on some incomprehensible woe, and waited for someone to come in and begin to talk to them. (*Mountain*, 179)

Merton remained fascinated by Lax and tried repeatedly to understand and describe his complicated personality:

To name Robert Lax in another way, he was a kind of combination of Hamlet and Elias. A potential prophet, but without rage. A king, but a Jew too. A mind full of tremendous and subtle intuitions, and every day he found less and less to say about them, and resigned himself to being inarticulate. In his hesitations, though without embarrassment or nervousness at all, he would often curl his long legs all around a chair, in seven different ways, while he was trying to find a word with which to begin. He talked best sitting on the floor.

And the secret of his constant solidity I think has always been a kind of natural, instinctive spirituality, a kind of inborn direction to the living God. Lax has always been afraid he was in a blind alley, and half aware that, after all, it might not be a blind alley, but God, infinity.

He had a mind naturally disposed, from the very cradle, to a kind of affinity for Job and St. John of the Cross. And I now know that he was born so much of a contemplative that he will probably never be able to find out how much.

To sum it up, even the people who have always thought he was "too impractical" have always tended to venerate him — in the way people who value material security unconsciously venerate people who do not fear insecurity. (*Mountain*, 181)

Lax was a Jew, and in many respects he was a prophet for Merton. There is tremendous simplicity and power in their relationship. This becomes visible in a conversation they had walking on Sixth Avenue one spring evening. Merton recorded the conversation word for word:

Lax suddenly turned around and asked me the question:

L: "What do you want to be, anyway?"

M: "I don't know; I guess what I want is to be a good Catholic."

L: "What do you mean, you want to be a good Catholic? . . . What you should say . . . is that you want to be a saint."

M: "How do you expect me to become a saint?"

L: "By wanting to."

M: "I can't be a saint, I can't be a saint. . . ."

L: "All that is necessary to be a saint is to want to be one. Don't you believe that God will make you what He created you to be, if you will consent to let Him do it? All you have to do is desire it."

The next day I told Mark Van Doren:

"Lax is going around saying that all a man needs to be a saint is to want to be one."

"Of course," said Mark.

All these people were much better Christians than I. They understood God better than I. What was I doing? Why was I so slow, so mixed up, still, so uncertain in my directions and so insecure? (*Mountain*, 237–38)

Later, when Merton stood in the monk's choir in the Trappist abbey, he discovered Lax among the guests. When they got together Lax told him that he had become a Catholic. When Lax was teaching at the University of North Carolina, his friend Rice had written him: "Come to New York and we will find a priest and ask him to baptize you." Merton wrote:

All of a sudden, after all those years of debating back and forth, Lax just got on a train and went to New York. Nobody had ever put the matter up to him like that before.... They found a Jesuit in that big church up on Park Avenue and he baptized him, and that was that.

Of all the people Merton knew in his youth, Lax was undoubtedly the man closest to him. But if that is true, then we can also see how much respect Merton had for him. Lax was his best friend, but he never used him to avoid his deepest feelings of solitude. He describes him more as one of the signs on the way to God.

Perhaps it is indeed a very important aspect of Merton's contemplative spirit that he remained detached from his environment, even from his good friends. He loved them, but didn't use them; he was intensely thankful for everything he received from them, but he didn't attach himself to them. More and more he learned to see his friends as signposts toward God. The power of friendship is great if it doesn't find all of its meaning in itself. If people expect too much from each other, they can do each other harm; and disappointment and bitterness can overpower love and even replace it. Already as a student in New York, Merton didn't try to avoid solitude. While his friends were often busy with all sorts of activities, he sought out a quiet place for prayer. In this silence he got to know God and also learned to value and admire his friends. Lax, in fact, meant so much to Merton because he found in him just what he had discovered in silence. Merton could call Lax a born mystic only because he himself had experienced God as the one who spoke to him in silence.

It is this silence that became fuller and deeper for Merton, first as a member of a monastic community, then as a hermit. It is important to see that it is this experience of God in silence that put Merton more and more in a position to recognize both God and the devil in people and events around him.

The silence prepared him to understand everything he saw as a possible sign on the way to a new world.

Events

We have described books and people as signs on the way to silence. The more we reflect on this, the clearer it becomes that we cannot really understand God's work with humanity. In the final analysis people do not explain much to us. They are but signs that lead us to suspect something unspeakably great.

This is also true for the events about which we now want to speak. Millions have experienced these same events, but for Merton they became signs on the way. Here we refer specifically to the Second World War. A year after it broke out, in 1939, Merton entered the Trappists. The premonitions of the war and the ominous beginning preoccupied him intensely.

His diaries make this very clear, and in his novel *My Argument with the Gestapo,* the problem of war and peace is central. How personal a thing it was for Merton appears in the characterization that he himself gave to his novel: a "sardonic meditation on the world in which I then found myself: an attempt to define its predicament and my own place in it" (*Argument,* 6).

The atmosphere of war had a deep influence on Merton and probably hastened his way to the abbey. The war forced him to pose the fundamental question that otherwise may have long remained suppressed: "How can I be a man of peace?" He began to understand more clearly the gripping power of destruction all around him as an invitation to voluntarily become nothing. The craving to conquer more land and more goods became for him an invitation to voluntarily take his distance from all possessions and to go naked through life. The blind violence that tore the world from its joints became for him an appeal to follow the path of nonviolence and to accept all the consequences.

On June 16, 1940, he wrote in his diary:

> Therefore, if I don't pretend, like other people, to understand the war, I do know this much: that the knowledge of what is going on only makes it seem desperately important to be voluntarily poor, to get rid of all possessions this instant. I am scared, sometimes, to own anything, even a name, let alone a coin, or shares in the oil, the munitions, the airplane factories. I am scared to take a proprietary interest in anything, for fear that my love of what I own may be killing somebody somewhere.
>
> (*Journal*, 98)

A year later, after Merton had his first extended contact with Trappist life, this insight became deeper. He began to see more clearly that self-imposed poverty not only prevents violence, but also makes one completely free to work in the middle of danger. Detachment in poverty is more than a means to prevent one's fellow men and women from suffering conscious or unconscious violence. It also offers the unheard-of chance to stand without fear in a violent world. This is the new insight that already appeared in the novel he wrote in the summer of 1941. To the question of whether he is afraid in this dangerous world, the main character, Merton himself, answers:

> I know I am in danger, but how can I be afraid of danger? If I remember I am nothing, I will know the danger can take nothing from me.... Yes, I am afraid, because I forget that I am nothing. If I remembered that I have nothing called my own that will not be lost anyway, that only what is not mine but God's will ever live, then I would not fear so many false fears. (*Argument*, 138)

Here a new life ideal becomes visible. Detachment does not mean shirking one's responsibilities. Rather it is a supremely active deed that makes it possible to move unprejudiced and unafraid into the center of the evil. The poor person can enter into this center with nonviolence because she has nothing to defend and she can destroy evil at its root.

The self-emptied person is revolutionary in the real sense because he claims nothing — not even his life — as his possession, and therefore he can take away the false basis of war and violence by refusing every compromise with possessions.

We find the start of these thoughts in the young Merton, who searches for his answer to the Second World War. It is therefore not surprising that we see Merton later as one of the most important writers on nonviolence, as one of the best interpreters of Gandhi, and as the one who constantly questions what *kenosis* (self-emptying) means for the modern man or woman.

Books, people, and events: We have described these as signs on the way to silence. They do not give an explanation of his call, but are only symptoms of it. Gilson, Huxley, John of the Cross, Therese of Lisieux, Ignatius of Loyola — Merton discovered them in literature and experimented with their ideas. Mark Van Doren, Daniel Walsh, Bramachari, and Bob Lax — Merton met them in New York and experienced God's love in their friendship. The events of the Second World War — they formed the context in which he read the books and met the people, supported his vague premonitions, and quickened his personal decision.

It is perhaps always a bit disappointing when we look for an answer to the question of God in our lives. We are left only with titles of books, names of people, and a few old facts. It all seems a bit lean and superficial. We cannot capture God in titles, names, and facts, but many things hint at and point to God. And therefore it is only the one who prays to God, quite possibly the one who searches for silence, who can recognize God in the many little ideas, meetings, and happenings on the way.

FOR MEDITATION

Dialogue 4: With candles on the altar

C: You who went away from here [England] lost, would you ever have returned here if you had been lost still?

M: I make this journey for the reasons Dante made his.

C: Are you an exile, stranger?

M: Yes, I am an exile all over the earth.

C: You who have wanted to return to the midst of this fire and penance, for Dante's reasons, are you afraid that you are in danger, in this hostile country?

M: I know I am in danger, but how can I be afraid of danger? If I remember I am nothing, I will know the danger can take nothing from me.

C: And yet, are you afraid of the danger?

M: Yes, I am afraid, because I forget that I am nothing. If I remembered that I have nothing called my own that will not be lost anyway, that only what is not mine but God's will ever live, then I would not fear so many false fears.

(*Argument*, 137–38)

Chapter Three

Conquering Solitude

Thomas Merton wrote about himself in the years before he became a Trappist as if he were writing about a journalist, not only because he was writing for different magazines, but also because for him the concept "journalist" had a particular meaning. This appears most clearly in his novel *My Argument with the Gestapo,* in which he himself is the main character. He comes back to a bombed-out London where he had lived as a student. He appears there as a journalist, but not in the sense that the people around him think of a journalist. To be sure, he observes and reports. He is in the thick of the happenings. He writes down what he hears, sees, smells, and tastes. But the question "What is important?" has a different meaning for him than for his colleagues who must provide the home front with news. He is a journalist, a reporter, but a journalist who stops at everyday things and asks what their sense and meaning are. The terrible suffering, death, and destruction he sees are new for him in the sense that they formulate in a completely new way the question of the meaning of life and death. The opinions of police and military are no explanation for him; peace conferences and armistices are no real signs of hope.

Merton's questions are: What is peace? What is justice? What is love? Are we ready for this? And especially, What is *my* place in the middle of this chaotic and noisy world? This last question led him to the silence of Gethsemani. In this silence, where he lived for twenty-seven years, he in fact remained a journalist, a reporter who observed the world in which he lived, but under the critical eye of the Gospel.

The Diaries

In the years Merton spent in the Trappist monastery, he wrote an enormous amount — at least thirty-five books and an impressive number of articles, not to mention the many works (such as journals and letters) that have appeared posthumously. When we look at all this work, it appears that the great power of Merton as a writer still remains in his ability to comment on the concrete happenings of the day, and to do this out of a contemplative silence. He never wrote great systematic works, and his most objective work is his weakest. Therefore, in the long run his diaries and his short commentaries may prove to belong to his most important contributions.

In Gethsemani Merton wrote many diaries, two of which are *The Sign of Jonas,* covering the years 1942–52, and *Conjectures of a Guilty Bystander,* which he kept during the years 1956–65. We must look to them for an understanding of how he grew in his newly acquired solitude.

In many respects *The Sign of Jonas* is a monologue, in which Merton — finally a Trappist — now really tries to conquer the solitude to which he was led by many signs. It is an impressive book because it describes the painful wrestling of humanity with God. And, in a very convincing manner, it demonstrates that the walls of an abbey are certainly no guarantee for solitude and inner silence. But this all means that Merton himself in many instances stands in the center of *The Sign of Jonas.* It is an honest, but also anxious, adventure in self-revelation and self-discovery. Up to now the question was: Where is my place in the world? The answer was, "in solitude." Now the question is: What is my place in solitude? This has been the subject of a long struggle, written down in a diary that on first reading may seem boring, but on further study illustrates an exceptionally fascinating development.

His second diary, *Conjectures of a Guilty Bystander,* is completely different in its style and content. Merton calls it "a personal version of the world in the 1960s." He writes:

These notes . . . are an implicit dialogue with other minds, a dialogue in which questions are raised. But do not expect to find "my answers." I do not have clear answers to current questions. I do have questions, and, as a matter of fact, I think a man is known better by his questions than by his answers. (*Conjectures*, v)

The subject of this diary is not Merton himself but his reactions to the books he read, the people he spoke with, and the events he heard about. The titles of the parts of the two diaries show a clear difference. In *The Sign of Jonas*, the parts are called: Solemn Profession, Death of an Abbot, Major Orders, and To the Altar of God. In *Conjectures of a Guilty Bystander* we find other titles such as: Earth's Dream, Truth and Violence, The Madman Runs to the East, and so on.

This development is very important. Just as we can enter into a real intimate relation with one another only when we first get to know our own identities, often after much pain and suffering, so Merton was really in the position to occupy himself critically with his world only after he had found his own solitude. *The Sign of Jonas* can in many ways be described as the adolescence of a contemplative, in which the spiritual identity crisis must be brought to a solution. As often as people venture to a deeper, more fundamental level of life in trying to give form to their lives, they expose themselves to an ever more painful and heartrending crisis. In this sense people have just as many adolescences as they take risks to *fathom* their life.

Once God has called you to solitude,
everything you touch leads you
further into solitude.
—Merton

Solitude can be sought and found
in the routine of the simple world,
in which one can be alone in one's heart.
—Nouwen

Shortly before his death, Thomas Merton was asked by the Holy See to collaborate on a message to the world on the meaning of the contemplative life. Merton had no time for a systematic description, but answered immediately with a personal letter, which was widely publicized. In this he said:

> The contemplative has nothing to tell you except to reassure you and say that if you dare to penetrate your own silence and dare to advance without fear into the solitude of your own heart, and risk the sharing of that solitude with the lonely other who seeks God through you and with you, then you will truly recover the light and the capacity to understand what is beyond words and beyond explanations because it is too close to be explained: It is the intimate union in the depths of your own heart, of God's spirit and your own secret inmost self, so that you and He are in all truth One Spirit.
>
> (Letter, August 21, 1967)

These words, which seem so simple and obvious, were written against a background of a life's journey in which they had become the flesh and blood of the one who wrote them. Thus, the conquering of silence and solitude by Merton is also of real importance in understanding his role in the discussion of violence and nonviolence and in appreciating his contribution to the dialogue with the Eastern mystics.

If we now want to look further into Thomas Merton's strug-
gles for solitude, we must begin with the sober statement that
Thomas Merton, who entered the Trappists to find rest and
silence, in fact ended up in a particularly busy, restless, and
noisy situation. The World War had confronted not only Merton but also many other young Americans, who had come to
know the world from its cruelest side, with the question of the
meaning of existence. The result was that in the years 1940–
50 the Abbey of Gethsemani grew from 70 to 270 members.
Merton comments, a little sourly, "Thus two hundred and
seventy lovers of silence and solitude are all packed into a
building that was built for seventy" (*Sign*, 14).

That meant new training courses, new buildings, the preparation for new foundations, and so forth; much talk and
debate, many discussions and lectures, many tractors and bull-
dozers, and the constant going in and coming out of busy
monks. Merton called Gethsemani, in those days, a "furnace
of ambivalence."

In this context, then, we must also look at the question
that completely dominated the first part of *The Sign of Jonas*:
"Am I here in my place? Should I not enter the Carthusians,
or just become a common hermit?" This is a search for silence,
yet also the question of one whose inner turmoil made him
desire more hours of calm than the abbey could offer him at
that time.

The youthful enthusiasm and generosity with which he wanted to give himself to God without reservation were so frustrated that he thought he could never reach his vocation at Gethsemani. He wanted more solitude and more silence. But his own restlessness and his relatively busy life in the abbey made him wonder whether he was called to a purely contemplative life. His abbot and spiritual director encouraged him more and more to write. Meanwhile he had to do much work in the fields, and he received other jobs from all sides. In this situation he began to question whether his longing for solitude wasn't perhaps a self-seeking, egoistic desire. He wrote: "It is not important to live for contemplation, but for God." He began to question his motives and at the same time found his only foothold in obedience to his superiors, who said he was in his place in the abbey.

Compassionate Solitude

In this crisis a new light broke through. It was the discovery of the contemplative value of what seems common routine, and of the doubtful value of all feelings of delight and spiritual satisfaction. Solitude can be sought and found in the routine of the simple world, in which one can be alone in one's heart. "Today I seemed to be very much assured that solitude is indeed His will for me and that it is truly God Who is calling me into the desert. But this desert is not necessarily a geographical one. It is a solitude of heart in which created joys are consumed and reborn in God" (*Sign*, 59).

During this time Merton also made another discovery: that contemplation doesn't mean learning about contemplation; that silence isn't thinking, learning, and talking about silence; and that solitude doesn't mean a heartful of beautiful thoughts about being alone with God. With great honesty he uncovered his own intellectualism and his rational approach to his problems. He said to himself:

> Here is what you need to do more and more — shut up about all that — architecture, Spirit of the Order, contemplation, liturgy, chant — be simple and poor or you will never have any peace. Take what is atrocious without complaint, unless you are in some way officially bound to complain. Otherwise keep still. (*Sign*, 122–23)

At this time his temptation to become a Carthusian crept up in the background. But then, too, a new level of solitude was beginning to develop in him that he could put into words only with difficulty. It was a solitude that invited him to be no longer busy with himself, no longer concerned over what he did or had to do, no longer to want to hold in his own hands the way to solitude. At that moment, too, his vision of his vocation as an author changed. Instead of a handicap, his writing became an entrance to real silence and solitude.

Writing in fact became for him the only way to sanctity. "If I am to be a saint," he writes, "I must also put down on paper what I have become ... to put myself down on paper ... with the most complete simplicity and integrity, masking nothing" (*Sign*, 288–89).

In his work as a writer, Merton discovered also a new experience of poverty. By his writing he had made himself and his most inner feelings and thoughts a public possession. In this way he had disowned himself and allowed others to enter in his monastic silence. In this way his fame had made him spiritually poor. But this same poverty made the world around him appear to him in a new way. It seems as if everything belonged to him just when there was nothing left to him that he could call his private property. The air, the trees, the whole world were now singing the honor of God, and he felt fire and music in the earth under his feet. The beauty of creation made him poor and wealthy at the same time and gave him peace and happiness. This beauty kept him from wanting to experience nature as a possession, but helped him to deeply experience his silence and solitude.

But this solitude and rest were cruelly disturbed during a period of terrible anxiety and uncertainty. In December 1949, Merton wrote, desperate as a sick and depressed person who has lost his orientation and feels completely alienated from himself: "It is fear that is driving me into solitude" (*Sign*, 248). It seemed as if everything were broken to pieces and as if nothing were left of the beautiful contemplative ideals. "I am exhausted by fear," he wrote (*Sign*, 248). After eight years of life in the monastery, he felt miserable, sinful, guilty, and without any prospects. The solitude was now felt as harsh, difficult, and painful and gave him the experience of being empty and even totally "nothing."

But then, at the depth of his misery, he again found God and solidarity with other human beings. When everything was dark, he found himself in God's own solitude. In the winter of 1950 he wrote:

> Solitude is not merely a negative relationship. It is not merely the absence of people. True solitude is a participation in the solitariness of God — Who is in all things. His solitude is not a local absence but a metaphysical transcendence. (*Sign*, 262)

This heavy darkness appeared to be a purification that prepared him for a new task. In May 1951, Merton became the spiritual director for the students. That is the Sign of Jonas. God called Jonas to go to the people, but Jonas fled to solitude until God led him back through the whale to his real calling. Merton said then, too, "like Jonas himself, I find myself traveling toward my destiny in the belly of a paradox" (*Sign*, 21). But when he stood before his students, he discovered that something great had happened to him. The silence and solitude had buried themselves so deeply in his heart that he was in the position to take on a very deep and intimate relation with other persons. Perhaps most moving in *The Sign of Jonas* is the development of compassion in solitude. In silence Merton discovered humanity once again. The new name for the desert in which he saw many of his self-constructed ambitions destroyed was: *compassion.* He learned to feel and respect silence in the life of another. He learned there to love his monastic brothers, not for what they say but for what they are. He saw now, with amazement, the quietude and solitude that lived in them. Now he wanted only to be a man among people, a member of humanity.

The conquering of silence also gave him a new task: to share this silence with others. But that required no special effort because: "Once God has called you to solitude, everything you touch leads you further into solitude" (*Sign,* 323). And now Merton dared to write:

> What is my new desert? The name of it is *compassion.* There is no wilderness so terrible, so beautiful, so arid and so fruitful as the wilderness of compassion. It is the only desert that shall truly flourish like the lily.
>
> (*Sign,* 323)

In this deepest solitude that became compassion, one is no longer examined. Curiosity turns into admiration, direction turns into guidance, and silence becomes a place where no one has to ask questions, but all can really be together in God.

And so ends the first diary written in the abbey. Merton was the reporter of his own inner life. He put his daily feelings and thoughts under the critical eye of the Gospel, and in the depth of solitude he found God and other human beings. This cleansing was necessary before he could detach himself from his preoccupations to touch the world — which was being wrenched apart by racial discrimination, violence, and poverty — with the hand of compassion.

FOR MEDITATION

On traveling with Jonas

For me, the vow of stability has been the belly of the whale. I have always felt a great attraction to the life of perfect solitude. It is an attraction I shall probably never entirely lose. During my years as a student at Gethsemani, I often wondered if this attraction was not a genuine vocation to some other religious Order.... My own solution of this problem is the main theme of the present book. Like the prophet Jonas, whom God ordered to go to Nineveh, I found myself with an almost uncontrollable desire to go in the opposite direction. God pointed one way and all my "ideals" pointed in the other. It was when Jonas was traveling as fast as he could away from Nineveh, toward Tharsis, that he was thrown overboard, and swallowed by a whale who took him where God wanted him to go. . . . Like Jonas himself I find myself traveling toward my destiny in the belly of a paradox. (*Sign*, 20–21)

On vocation

The important thing is not to live for contemplation but to live for God. That is obvious, because, after all, that is the contemplative vocation. (*Sign*, 38)

On the noise of the day

You have made my soul for Your peace and Your silence, but it is lacerated by the noise of my activity and my desires. My mind is crucified all day by its own hunger for experience, for ideas, for satisfaction. And I do not possess my house in silence. (*Sign*, 54)

On shutting up

What is the use of my complaining about not being a contemplative, if I do not take the opportunities I get for contemplation? I suppose I take them, but in the wrong way. I spend the time looking for something to read about contemplation — something to satisfy my raffish spiritual appetite — instead of shutting up and emptying my mind and leaving the inner door open for the Holy Spirit to enter from the inside, all the doors being barred and all my blinds down. (*Sign*, 76)

On writing

I am finding myself forced to admit that my lamentations about my writing job have been foolish. At the moment, the writing is one thing that gives me access to some real silence and solitude. Also I find that it helps me to pray, because when I pause at my work I find that the mirror inside me is surprisingly clean and deep and serene and God shines there and is immediately found, without hunting, as if He had come close to me while I was writing and I had not observed His coming. And this, I think, should be the cause of great joy, and to me it is. (July 21, 1949, *Sign*, 204–5)

On reading Scripture

By the reading of Scripture I am so renewed that all nature seems renewed around me and with me. The sky seems to be a pure, a cooler blue, the trees a deeper green, light is sharper on the outlines of the forest and the hills and the whole world is charged with the glory of God and I feel fire and music in the earth under my feet. (*Sign*, 212)

On the futility of words

It does no good to use big words to talk about Christ. Since I seem to be incapable of talking about Him in the language of a child, I have reached the point where I can scarcely talk about Him at all. All my words fill me with shame. (*Sign*, 222)

On being alone

And now, for the first time, I began to know what it means to be *alone*. Before becoming a priest I had made a great fuss about solitude and had been rather a nuisance to my superiors and directors in my aspirations for a solitary life. Now, after my ordination, I discovered that the essence of a solitary vocation is that it is a vocation to fear, to helplessness, to isolation in the invisible God. Having found this, I now began for the first time in my life to taste a happiness that was so complete and so profound that I no longer needed to reflect upon it. There was no longer any need to remind myself that I was happy — a vain expedient to prolong a transient joy — for this happiness was real and permanent and even in a sense eternal. It penetrated to the depths below consciousness, and in all storms, in all fears, in the deepest darkness, it was always unchangeably there. (*Sign*, 227)

Otherwise — feeling of fear, dejection, nonexistence. Yet it gives me a kind of satisfaction to realize that it is not by contact with any other creature that I can recover the sense that I am real. Solitude means being lonely not in a way that pleases you but in a way that frightens and empties you to the extent that it means being exiled even from yourself.

(*Sign*, 243)

It is in deep solitude that I find the gentleness with which I can truly love my brothers. The more solitary I am, the more affection I have for them. It is pure affection, and filled with reverence for the solitude of others. Solitude and silence teach me to love my brothers for what they are, not for what they say. (*Sign*, 261)

On interior silence

When you gain this interior silence you can carry it around with you in the world, and pray everywhere. But just as interior asceticism cannot be acquired without concrete and exterior mortification, so it is absurd to talk about interior silence where there is no exterior silence. (*Sign*, 302)

On forest glory

When your tongue is silent, you can rest in the silence of the forest. When your imagination is silent, the forest speaks to you, tells you of its unreality and of the Reality of God. But when your mind is silent, then the forest suddenly becomes magnificently real and blazes transparently with the Reality of God: for now I know that the Creation which first seems to reveal Him, in concepts, then seems to hide Him, by the same concepts, finally is *revealed in Him*, in the Holy Spirit: and we who are in God find ourselves united, in Him, with all that springs from Him. This is prayer, and this is glory!

(*Sign*, 332)

On the God of night

God, my God, God Whom I meet in darkness, with You it is always the same thing! Always the same question that nobody knows how to answer! (*Sign*, 342)

Lord God of this great night: do You see the woods? Do You hear the rumor of their loneliness? Do You behold their secrecy? Do You remember their solitudes? Do You see that my soul is beginning to dissolve like wax within me? (*Sign*, 350)

On meditative prayer

What is the use of praying if at the very moment of prayer, we have so little confidence in God that we are busy planning our own kind of answer to our prayer? (*Thoughts*, 36)

In meditative prayer, one thinks and speaks not only with his mind and lips, but in a certain sense with his *whole being.* Prayer is then not just a formula of words, or a series of desires springing up in the heart — it is the orientation of our whole body, mind, and spirit to God in silence, attention, and adoration. All good meditative prayer is *a conversion of our entire self to God* (*Thoughts*, 48).

On the spiritual life

If you want to have a spiritual life you must unify your life. A life is either all spiritual or not spiritual at all. No man can serve two masters. (*Thoughts*, 55)

My life is a listening. His is a speaking. My salvation is to hear and respond. For this, my life must be silent. Hence, my silence is my salvation. (*Thoughts*, 72)

A *prayer*

My Lord God, I have no idea where I am going, I do not see the road ahead of me, I cannot know for certain where it will end. Nor do I really know myself, and the fact that I think I am following your will does not mean that I am actually doing so. But I believe that the desire to please you does in fact please you. And I hope I have that desire in all that I am doing. I hope that I will never do anything apart from that desire. And I know that if I do this you will lead me by the right road, though I may know nothing about it. Therefore I will trust you always though I may seem to be lost and in the shadow of death. I will not fear, for you are ever with me, and you will never leave me to face my perils alone. (*Thoughts*, 81)

On *where we find God*

[God] is found when He is sought and when He is no longer sought He escapes us. He is heard only when we hope to hear Him, and if, thinking our hope to be fulfilled, we cease to listen, He ceases to speak, His silence ceases to be vivid and becomes dead, even though we recharge it with the echo of our own emotional noise (*Thoughts*, 86).

Let me seek, then, the gift of silence, and poverty, and solitude, where everything I touch is turned into prayer: where the sky is my prayer, the birds are my prayer, the wind in the trees is my prayer, for God is all in all (*Thoughts*, 91).

Chapter Four

Unmasking the Illusion

Above one of the doors of the abbey, the words "God alone" are carved in the stone. That was what Merton wanted — away from the wild business of the hustling world, which sought happiness where it couldn't be found. Away from the many discussions and defenses and arguments over things that didn't go any further than self-interest. Away from the novels, reports, and stories with which he had wanted to make himself popular. Away from the movies and bars that numbed the senses and the source of life. Away into the silence of the abbey, the rest of nature, the regularity of the prayer life, to be with "God alone."

But this romantic life, in which a real seeking for God lay hidden, couldn't remain romantic for very long. It is fascinating to read how Thomas Merton is followed his whole life long with the rumor that he had left the monastery, that he had not persevered, that he was no longer a monk or a priest, that he was married or had disappeared to another country. Already when *The Seven Storey Mountain* was published, it was said that he would soon leave, and Merton was constantly tormented by the sick hope of some of his readers that he would not persevere. To many, remaining in a monastery sounded too beautiful, too pious, too sensational. Even many of the faithful suggested that for a romantic such as Merton it was impossible to persevere in any monastery, especially in a Trappist community.

Perhaps there was still a kernel of truth in all these reports, insofar as Merton indeed had to be purified in solitude to become a real monk. The "God alone" had first to be shaken from all traces of false romanticism and of flight from the evil world in order to really be able to bear fruit. In *The Sign of Jonas* we find a part of this purification described. Soon he learned to see that becoming a Carthusian would not help him in his search for real solitude and silence, that solitude is primarily a quality of the heart, and that solitude would become false when its social dimension is not recognized.

Social Solitude

Perhaps Merton's most important discovery was the discovery of others at the depths of his own solitude. He experienced a new solidarity in the depths of his silence, and he seemed to find there, where he was most alone, the basis of community. In silence his mockery became generosity, his self-conceit became solidarity, and his sarcasm became compassion. On

March 3, 1951, when he had been in Gethsemani for ten years, he wrote about his life in solitude:

And now I owe everyone else in the world a share in that life. My first duty is to start, for the first time, to live as a member of a human race which is no more (and no less) ridiculous than I am myself. And my first human act is the recognition of how much I owe everybody else.

(*Sign*, 312)

Through purification and solitude, "God alone" became "together with all people." In silence Merton discovered that being a monk is preeminently a social calling. This conviction became more mature after 1951, when Merton became spiritual director for the students. In the 1960s when racial strife burst loose in all its vehemence, when the conscience of America suffered under Vietnam, and when poverty became more apparent, Merton was one of the most influential voices to which people listened in order to find some light in the darkness and some clarity in the midst of the confusion of spirit.

On December 10, 1968, a few hours before his death, Merton gave a lecture in Bangkok on Marxism and Monasticism. In this he recounted:

I was at a meeting to which many revolutionary university leaders from France, Italy, Germany, the Low

Countries, had been invited. This meeting took place in Santa Barbara, California.... In a lull between conferences I was speaking informally with some of those students, and I introduced myself as a monk, and one of the French revolutionary students immediately said: "We are monks also...." The monk is essentially someone who takes up a critical attitude towards the contemporary world and its structures.... But the criticism is undoubtedly quite different.... The student seemed to be alluding to the fact that if one is to call himself in one way or another a monk he must have in some way or other reached some kind of critical conclusion about the validity of certain claims made by secular society and its structures with regard to the end of man's existence. ("Marxist Theory and Monastic Theories," 2)

This story displays Merton's deep conviction that contemplation is basically a social matter, and that silence, solitude, and prayer are not private properties, but belong to the people with and for whom he lives. His conviction that solitude didn't belong to him as a possession came forth out of his heart-rending discovery that Auschwitz, Hiroshima, Vietnam, and Watts were present in the intimate core of his own being. There, where he thought he could be alone with himself, he found that he wasn't one man, but that in him lived human-kind, in all its misery but also in its longing for love. And out of this self-examination, the call came forth to put into words his own deepest experience and to offer it to others for reflection, because this experience wasn't a private matter; rather, it was often the unspoken and unreflected experience of all humanity.

How Merton personally experienced this appears in the fact that his own historical circumstance reveals itself to him as a heavy obligation.

> That I should have been born in 1915, that I should be the contemporary of Auschwitz, Hiroshima, Vietnam, and the Watts riots are things about which I was not first consulted. Yet they are also events in which, whether I like it or not, I am deeply and personally involved.
>
> (*Contemplation*, 145)

This experience brought Merton to the conviction that a choice was being demanded of him. If his own history contained a calling, he could accept it or throw it off. And the tragedy is that religious, monks, Christians threaten to repudiate their calling under the mantle of scorning the world. He wrote:

> To choose the world is ... first of all an acceptance of a task and a vocation in the world, in history and in time. And it has now become transparently obvious that

mere automatic "rejection of the world" and "contempt for the world" is in fact not a choice but the evasion of choice. The man who pretends that he can turn his back on Auschwitz or Vietnam and act as if they were not there is simply bluffing. I think that this is getting to be generally admitted, even by monks.

(*Contemplation*, 149)

But for Merton these thoughts in no way meant that he now would be better off to leave Gethsemani in order to actively engage in the civil rights or peace movements, to take part in demonstrations, to support draft resisters, and to sound his protesting voice everywhere. So thought his readers, who felt that someone who thought and wrote as Merton did belonged in the front line of the action and not in the garden of a monastery. But on this very point he was not understood. In one of his last letters from India, he still found it necessary to write: "I hope there are not too many crazy rumors. Keep telling everyone that I am a monk of Gethsemani and intend to remain one all my days" (Asian Letters, 1968).

In this light it is even more important to understand the kind of rebellion to which Merton wanted to dedicate himself. His vocation as monk was neither to fight on the front lines nor to turn his back on the world with contempt. His task was not the denial of a reality, but the unmasking of an illusion. He wrote:

The world as pure object is something that is not there. It is not a reality outside us for which we exist.... It is a living and self-creating mystery of which I am myself a part, to which I am myself, my own unique door. When I find the world in my own ground, it is impossible for me to be alienated by it. (*Contemplation*, 154–55).

Merton understood that the unmasking of illusion belonged to the essence of the contemplative life. The many years of prayer and solitude had confronted him with his own illusions. But through this he was also prepared to show himself and his fellow human beings that which they would rather keep hidden. This unmasking is not a game one can choose to play or not to play. It is a sacred duty and regards the here and now of what occurs in this world. In his *Seeds of Destruction*, where he reveals himself as a sharp critic of society, he wrote:

We are bound to search "history," that is to say the intelligible actions of men, for some indications of their inner significance, and some relevance to our commitment as Christians. (*Seeds*, 18)

In the years 1960–68 "history" meant for Merton: the killing of children in Birmingham and civil rights workers in Mississippi; the killing of Mrs. Liuzzo and the Unitarian minister in Selma, Alabama; the burning of churches in the

Nonviolence implies a kind of bravery
far different from violence.
—Merton

Merton had discovered
the possibility of a compassion
that in essence is nonviolent.
—Nouwen

South and the riots in Watts, Newark, Chicago, and Cleveland; the long march from Selma to Montgomery and the dramatic march to Washington where Martin Luther King spoke of his dream. These were events that followed upon each other in quick succession and threatened the unity of a great land.

In 1963 President Kennedy was assassinated; in 1964–65 African American leaders were killed by snipers. The figure of Dr. King came forward as a sign of hope, and thousands walked with him in nonviolent protest. But when he was assassinated in 1968 and buried in Atlanta, nonviolence seemed to be buried with him, and black power alone remained as an alternative.

The hot summer of 1968 began with fires in Detroit and Chicago and a growing fear of chaos. In June 1968, Robert Kennedy was assassinated — the one white leader who still gave hope to African Americans. And after this the country fell lame and tired, waiting for a restoration that would give power to continue the battle with a much greater vehemence. Murder, hatred, anarchy, chaos, desperation, despair, a people full of anxiety — these were the signs of America. In every subway in New York police officers walked; taxi drivers refused to ride through certain areas after sundown. Parents did not dare let their children go alone to school. Meanwhile there came more factories, chimneys, and cars, covering the cities with a reddish-brown haze and threatening the health of their inhabitants. About all this Merton said: "We are bound to search the intelligible actions of men, for some indications of their inner significance" (*Seeds,* 18).

It would be unfair to say that Merton had an exclusive interest in the racial question. He was passionately interested in his whole world, and that meant for him the racial question, as well as international politics, the student protests, conscientious objection to war, and the many peace movements. He was interested in these current problems, not as one who might take part in an action group, but in order to search in his own silence for the inner meaning and message that they held for the Christian.

In a letter written in the summer of 1968 he summarized his convictions when he wrote:

I am against war, against violence, against violent revolution, for peaceful settlement of differences, for nonviolent but nevertheless radical changes. Change is needed, and violence will not really change anything: at most it will only transfer power from one set of bullheaded authorities to another. If I say these things, it is not because I am more interested in politics than in the Gospel. I am not. But today more than ever the Gospel commitment has political implications, because you cannot claim to be "for Christ" and espouse a political cause that implies callous indifference to the needs of millions of human beings and even cooperate in their destruction. (Midsummer Letter, 1968)

That was tough language for a monk, but for Merton it was necessary language in order to be a monk and remain one. He could speak this language because he had been able to test his experiences in solitude with what he saw and read about the times. Undoubtedly, the racial questions stood in the center, but precisely because he judged this struggle not from a strategic political point of view but from his experience of the gospel. His criticism took on a dimension that went far above the interests of a state or country. For he was concerned here once again with the unmasking of human illusions and not merely with some ideological standpoint.

James Baldwin

Merton's vision of the racial problem is most sharply expressed in his book *Seeds of Destruction*, especially in his "Letters to a White Liberal." Some deeper reflections of his attitude reside in his introduction to a number of texts of Gandhi, published under the title *Gandhi on Non-Violence*. These two studies deserve particular attention because they give us a good introduction to Merton as a critic of society.

In order to better understand Merton's unmasking of the illusion we must put two figures in the foreground — James

Baldwin and Mahatma Gandhi. Both figures had a great influence on Merton and prepared him to put into words what he had experienced in silence. James Baldwin is the African American author who in his books *Go Tell It on the Mountain,* *Another Country,* and *The Fire Next Time* shows in a shocking manner that the "black problem" in fact is a problem of white people. In a letter to Baldwin, Merton said:

> I recognize in conscience that I have a duty to try to make my fellow whites stop doing things they do and see the problem in a different light. (*Seeds,* 210)

Baldwin showed him that different light, and much that Merton said about the racial question was influenced by his ideas. In his "Letters to a White Liberal," Merton addresses himself with frightening sharpness to the progressive citizen who was in favor of integration.

> Now, my liberal friend, here is your situation. You, the well-meaning liberal, are right in the middle of all this confusion. You are, in fact, a political catalyst. On the other hand, with your good will and your ideals, your fine hopes and your generous, but vague, love of mankind in the abstract and of rights enthroned on a juridical Olympus, you offer a certain encouragement to the Negro (and you do right, my only complaint being that you are not yet right enough) so that, abetted by you,

he is emboldened to demand concessions. Though he knows you will not support all his demands, he is well aware that you will be forced to support some of them in order to maintain your image of yourself as a liberal. He also knows, however, that your material comforts, your security, and your congenial relations with the establishment are much more important to you than your rather volatile idealism, and that when the game gets rough you will be quick to see your own interests menaced by his demands. And you will sell him down the river for the five hundredth time in order to protect yourself. For this reason, as well as to support your own self-esteem, you are very anxious to have a position of leadership and control in the Negro's fight for rights, in order to be able to apply the brakes when you feel it is necessary.

(*Seeds*, 33–34)

Merton thought about the situation in his own land in all its consequences. The roots of destruction and violence lay in the white people themselves.... As long as white people don't want to look deeply into their own heart and turn into themselves, all their good intentions for African Americans will remain only flirtations, and all their so-called help only apparent concessions. An oppressed people cannot be controlled very long with artificial means, and it might just be that white liberals, who want to help everyone but will not change themselves, in fact are preparing the way for revolution. For it is just such white people who at a certain moment will say, "but now we are going too far," and instead of nonviolent Christians they will become violent fascists. Merton saw it in somber colors:

> At the end of this chain of thought I visualize you, my liberal friend, goose-stepping down Massachusetts Avenue in the uniform of an American Totalitarian Party in a mass rally where nothing but the most uproarious approval is manifest, except, by implication, on the part of silent and strangely scented clouds of smoke drifting over from the new "camps" where the "Negroes are living in retirement." (*Seeds*, 38)

The white Americans who speak with horror about the persecution of the Jews are at the point of setting up their own concentration camps because they refuse to recognize the evil in their land and come to conversion. The sense of the nonviolent protest of African Americans is not to give them a place in a corrupt society that they themselves have condemned to death, but to wake up the conscience of whites and to confront them with their own injustice and sin. Merton observed the irony of the situation. The Negro:

> is offering the white man a "message of salvation," but the white man is so blinded by his self-sufficiency and

self-conceit that he does not recognize the peril in which
he puts himself by ignoring the offer. (*Seeds,* 53)

Where do white people earn the conceit to think that
African Americans want to adopt their values and ideas? The
African American is sent as a prophet who is unrecognized.
Merton wrote:

[The Negro] is warning us that we cannot do without
him, and that if we insist on regarding him as an enemy,
an object of contempt or a rival, we will perhaps sterilize
and ruin our own lives. He is telling us that unless we
can enter into a vital and Christian relationship with
him, there will be hate, violence, and civil war indeed:
and from this violence perhaps none of us will emerge
whole. (*Seeds,* 52–53)

The fires, destruction, death, and riots are a *kairos,* a his-
toric opportunity for white people to finally confess their guilt
and to convert themselves. If they do not understand their
time as *kairos* and reject the offer of blacks, only revolution, violence, and destruction can follow, and the period
of nonviolence will be followed by a disastrous explosion of
violence.

Merton wrote this in 1963 when "Black Power" did not
exist. The well-known American church historian Martin E.
Marty attacked him vociferously. How did a monk, someone

sitting safely behind the walls of a Trappist monastery, dare to take on the robe of a prophet and predict a period of violence? But in the summer of 1967, when the American cities were in flames and Stokely Carmichael had launched his Black Power movement, Marty wrote that the monk Merton understood the situation of his country more deeply and fundamentally than he himself, and he offered a public apology for his rash criticism.

Merton didn't even think about saying, "You see, I was right." On the contrary, in 1968, he was still hopeful. He spoke then of the last chance that white people were being offered. But then a few blacks looted stores in an irrational frenzy and hurt themselves more than they did the whites. It seemed as if the summer of 1968 had taken away much of Merton's hope. Violence led to violence, and a police state seemed to be a definite possibility, one in which white extremists had the upper hand and would let their cruelty take free rein. That is the unmasking of the illusion of an integration without reform. Black people made white people see themselves by forcing them to draw the final consequences out of their hardness of heart. In this situation Merton could only hope against all hope:

> And I do hope we will keep our heads enough to pre-
> vent a complete polarization ... which makes all reason-
> able communication between the races impossible. ... If

Christianity is being discredited in the eyes of Negroes,
that does not dispense us from our duty to be authentic
Christians towards the Negro whether he likes us or not.

(*Faith,* 179)

This sounds like the voice of one who is a witness to the
bankruptcy of Christianity but refuses to give in to the temptation to deny the Lord. But Merton did not become bitter.
On the contrary, he knew he was dealing with a question that
penetrated so deeply into the core of human existence, where
good and evil find their sources, that every longing for a direct
visible result was a sign of little faith.

Bitterness is the reaction of one who expects something
from another without daring to look into his or her own heart,
and therefore becomes quickly disappointed. Merton knew
only too well that the sin, evil, and violence he found in the
world were the same sin, the same evil, and the same violence
he had discovered in his own heart through solitude, silence,
and prayer. The impurity in the world was a mirror of the
impurity in his own heart.

Gandhi

Perhaps as a result of the failure of nonviolence in the United
States, Merton became even more concerned with questions
of the interior life, concluding that nonviolence must quickly

degenerate into tactics and strategy when people still carry traces of violence in their heart. The only ones who have the right to speak about nonviolence are the ones who want to cleanse themselves of all violence through fasting, penance, and prayer. It was Baldwin who helped Merton to see that the "black problem," as it was so often referred to at the time, was essentially one of white people; it was Gandhi who cautioned him not to become a bitter idealist, and who taught him again and again to turn to his own interiority.

The teaching of Gandhi made a deep impression on Merton and influenced his thought strongly. Moreover it was Gandhi who set him on the path to the East. Merton wrote:

> The radical difference between him and other leaders, even the most sincere and honest of them, becomes evident by the fact that Gandhi is chiefly concerned with truth and with service, svadharma, rather than with the possible success of his tactics upon other people, and paradoxically it was his religious conviction that made Gandhi a great politician rather than a mere tactician or operator. (*Seeds*, 161)

It is easy to understand why Merton felt so much at home with Gandhi, when we consider that it was precisely in his solitude that Merton had discovered the possibility of a compassion that in essence is nonviolent. Nonviolence then, according to Merton, is not a method to achieve something that is already achieved. Baldwin had never said so, but only remarked that the blacks were nonviolent, not in order to conquer something, but in order to convert the white.

Merton saw now that nonviolence is not the searching for results but the inherent quality of spiritual unity. The creative spirit of unity that one can find in the silence of one's own heart is not a strictly personal possession, but the life of the spirit of all men and women. Therefore, releasing this spirit — which can also be called truth — is a service to all of humanity. That is not to say that one helps one's brothers and sisters by withdrawing in silence. For by seeking truth and justice together with other human beings, one can discover and free this truth in oneself.

One of the deepest of Merton's insights, which he formulated in the book *Gandhi on Non-Violence,* is that the spirit of truth is the spirit of nonviolence. The spirit of truth reveals to us that our present situation is not definitive but rather carries within itself the possibility of conversion to the good. Merton wrote:

Hence nonviolence implies a kind of bravery far different from violence. In the use of force, one simplifies the situation by assuming that the evil to be overcome is clear-cut, definite, and irreversible. Hence there remains but one thing: to eliminate it. Any dialogue with the sinner, any question of the irreversibility of his act, only means faltering and failure. Failure to eliminate evil is itself a defeat.... The greatest of tyrannies are all therefore based on the postulate that *there should never be any sin.* (*Gandhi,* 13–14)

Here Merton touched the core of nonviolence. Nonviolence stands or falls according to the vision of evil. If evil is seen only as an irreversible, clearly visible, and sharply outlined tumor, then there is only one possibility: cut it out. And then violence is necessary. But when evil is reversible and can be turned into good through forgiveness, then nonviolence becomes possible. Since Merton had experienced in his own life that forgiveness is possible through Christ, nonviolence became not only a possibility but also a prerequisite for being a Christian.

In a very impressive way, Merton showed how this nonviolence can give form to a new community. He said:

A violent change would not have been a serious change at all. To punish and destroy the oppressor is merely to initiate a new cycle of violence and oppression. The only real liberation is that which *liberates both the oppressor and the oppressed* at the same time from the same tyrannical automatism of the violent process which contains in itself the curse of irreversibility.... True freedom is then inseparable from the inner strength which can assume the common burden of evil which weighs both on oneself and one's adversary.... The highest form of spiritual freedom is, as Gandhi believed, to be sought in the strength of heart which is capable of liberating the oppressed and the oppressor together. . . . The oppressed must be able to be free within himself, so that he may begin to gain strength to pity his oppressor.

(*Gandhi*, 14–15)

Here we have come back to the compassion that must be formed in one's heart, a compassion that comes out of a deep experience of solidarity, in which one recognizes that the evil, sin, and violence one sees in the world and in the other are deeply rooted in one's own heart. Only when you want to confess this and want to rely on the merciful God who can bring good out of evil are you in a position to receive forgiveness and also to give it to other men and women who threaten you with violence. Precisely because Merton had discovered this nonviolent compassion in his solitude could he in a real sense be a monk — that is to say, one who unmasks through his criticism the illusions of a violent society and who wants to change the world in spirit and truth.

FOR MEDITATION

On overcoming racial division

As Christians, we must remember that in Christ there is no meaning to racial divisions. There is no white and black in

Christ: but if Christianity is being discredited in the eyes of Negroes, that does not dispense us from our duty to be authentic Christians toward the Negro whether he likes us or not. It is not our job to convince him that Christianity is "true" or "genuine," but to live up to what we ourselves profess to believe, so that we may not be judged by God for a mere lip-service that has (as we now begin to realize too late) reached the proportions of worldwide scandal. (*Faith*, 179)

On freedom from inner violence

[Political action for Gandhi] was not a means to acquire security and strength for one's self and one's party, but a means of witnessing to the truth and the reality of the cosmic structure by making one's own proper contribution to the order willed by God. One could thus preserve one's integrity and peace, being detached from results (which are in the hands of God) and being free from the inner violence that comes from division and untruth. (*Seeds*, 160)

Gandhi recognized, as no other world leader of our time has done, the necessity to be free from the pressures, the exorbitant and tyrannical demands of a society that is violent because it is essentially greedy, lustful and cruel. Therefore he fasted, observed days of silence, lived frequently in retreat, knew the value of solitude, as well as of the totally generous expenditure of his time and energy in listening to others and communicating with them. He recognized the impossibility of being a peaceful and nonviolent man if one submits passively to the insatiable requirements of a society maddened by overstimulation and obsessed with the demons of noise, voyeurism, and speed.

"Jesus died in vain," said Gandhi, "if he did not teach us to regulate the whole of life by the eternal law of love."

(Seeds, 163)

Chapter Five

Discovery of the East

In the preface to the Japanese edition of *The Seven Storey Mountain*, twenty years after the first publication of this "story of a conversion," Merton wrote that his motives for entering the Trappists were then strongly colored by negative feelings toward the world he was leaving. The emphasis lay on the break with, and the departure from, the sinful, egocentric, and money-hungry world. But since 1941 much had happened. He wrote in the preface:

> Since that time I have learned, I believe, to look back into that world with greater compassion, seeing those in it not as alien to myself, not as peculiar and deluded strangers, but as identified with myself. (*Mountain*, 9)

In silence his flight from people had become compassion for them. And after years of prayer and contemplation he found people again at the bottom of his solitude, people upon whom he had turned his back. This insight made him not only a highly respected spiritual leader of the students of Gethsemani but also an engaged critic of the events from 1960 to 1968, and one of the most outspoken proponents of nonviolence. Merton saw his monastery not only as a haven, where men sought to purify themselves so as to know God, but also as a center of spiritual action, from which he was to unmask the illusions of this world in a challenging way. The more he discovered the concrete demands of living, the less he emphasized living to purify himself.

> My monastery is not a home. It is not a place where I am rooted and established on the earth. It is not an environment in which I become aware of myself as an individual, but rather a place in which I disappear from the world as an object of interest in order to be everywhere in it by hiddenness and compassion.
>
> (*Mountain*, preface to the Japanese edition, 11)

But these words were written after twenty-five years of monastery life and were the fruit of a long search, both in the depths of his own soul and in the many often-shocking events of his day. In this new dialogue with the world, he had not only seen the sense and the necessity of a close involvement with the actualities but had also experienced the real limitations of this. In his book *Conjectures of a Guilty Bystander* he wrote:

> There is a time for action, a time for "commitment," but never for total involvement in the intricacies of a

movement. There is a moment of innocence and *kairos,* when action makes a great deal of sense. But who can recognize such moments? Not he who is debauched by a series of programs. And when all action has become absurd, shall one continue to act simply because once, a long time ago, it made a great deal of sense? As if one were always getting somewhere? There is a time to listen, in the active life as everywhere else, and the better part of action is waiting, not knowing what next, and not having a glib answer. (*Conjectures,* 156)

Merton himself had described the unrest of the civil rights fight as a *kairos,* a special time for the whites to pass over to action and to change their hearts. But he had also seen the powerlessness of a nonviolent resistance and the threatening rise of violence, and he had to admit that only his naked faith could give him hope when everything seemed dark.

The world about him looked like a desert. Merton lived in the midst of it but had the strength and power to remain true to the spirit of truth in himself. His belief in love and truth helped him remain involved in the social and political misery. But there was more. I recall a comment from John Eudes Bamberger, a monk and psychiatrist, who was both Merton's student and physician in Gethsemani. As Bamberger noted, one of Merton's characteristics that made him both a fascinating and an irritating personality was his capricious manner of judgment. He could sometimes assert seemingly contradictory things about a situation, one after the other. He first called the monastery his favorite home, and later he asserted that it was in fact no place where he could be rooted and established. In one conference he called Rilke the most fantastic poet of this century, and a few weeks later in another conference he said: "He was awfully limited" (*Continuum*, Summer 1969, 235).

Merton himself was conscious of this characteristic. In his introduction to *Seeds of Contemplation*, he warned readers not to stop with one strong statement, but to allow it to be relativized by another strong statement, which they would find elsewhere. It was this dialectic that once in a while led Merton into difficulties. The other monks could not always understand him, and the young monks he supervised were sometimes very confused by this feature of his teaching. When Merton on one day would assert exactly the opposite from the previous day, his listeners were irritated and said that they didn't know what he was worth.

This characteristic could suggest a cynicism that shunned every involvement, paralyzing a thought, an idea, or a suggestion by constantly asserting the opposite. Those who constantly say at the very moment they start to become enthusiastic, "But you can also look at it from the other side," will never get moving, and instead of guilty bystanders will become bitter cynics. But Merton did not become a cynic.

Does all our talk and discussion
about God bring us closer to him?
—Merton

In the way of thinking
that involves talking, discussing,
analyzing, and criticizing,
there is scarcely room for the God
who speaks whenever we are silent
and who comes in whenever
we have emptied ourselves.
—Nouwen

When he saw how the America of his time, uprooted by violence and confusion, was completely missing the chance of reform and was threatening to land in a dangerous polarization of power, he did not turn away in bitterness and disappointment. Instead he more and more went for advice to sages from the East, for whom contradictions and paradoxes do not lead to bitterness but to truth. He sought from them a better understanding of the situation of the West.

Therefore we now must turn to Merton's studies of the Chinese philosopher Chuang Tzu and Zen Buddhism in order to see how he perceived the relation between Buddhism and Christianity.

Chuang Tzu

The writer-philosopher Chuang Tzu had a very great influence on the thinking and feeling of Merton. He was one of the greatest Taoists during the flowering of Chinese philosophy, from 550 to 250 BC, and even today his thinking and spirit exercise a deeply penetrating influence on the different Zen schools in China and Japan.

What did Merton learn from Chuang Tzu? Nothing. Merton learned from him what Suzuki had said about Zen: "Zen teaches nothing; it merely enables us to wake up and become aware. It does not teach, it points" (*Zen*, 49–50). Merton added to this:

The acts and gestures of a Zen Master are no more "statements" than is the ringing of an alarm clock.

(*Zen*, 49–50)

In this sense Chuang Tzu is a real master for Merton: He taught him nothing new but awakened and led him through the barrier of his own inner contradictions to the deeper ground of his consciousness. It is therefore understandable that Merton wrote about his book *The Way of Chuang Tzu*: "I have enjoyed writing this book more than any other I can remember. . . . I simply like Chuang Tzu because he is what he is, and I feel no need to justify this liking to myself or to anyone else" (*Way*, 9–10). This is understandable because Chuang Tzu was, like Merton, a person who did not have to defend his own existence. Merton called Chuang Tzu a "subtle, funny, provoking thinker who doesn't easily put one over on you." John Eudes Bamberger says rightly that Chuang Tzu was a mirror-image of Merton, and whenever Merton defends his interest in Chuang Tzu, it often seems like a self-defense.

The key to the thought of Chuang Tzu is then, at the same time, a key to understanding Merton. This seems abundantly clear when Merton describes this key as:

. . . the complementarity of opposites, and this can be seen only when one grasps the central "pivot" of Tao which passes squarely through both "Yes" and "No," "I"

and "Not-I." Life is a continual development. All beings
are in a state of flux. Chuang Tzu would have agreed
with Herakleitos. What is impossible today may suddenly
become possible tomorrow. What is good and pleasant
today may, tomorrow, become evil and odious. What
seems right from one point of view may, when seen from
a different aspect, manifest itself as completely wrong.

(*Way*, 30)

These words are of great importance not only because Merton had experienced great contradictions in himself, not only
because he had discovered in people and events that he studied the most dramatic contradictions, but especially because
he himself had noticed that what is today a sensible reaction,
tomorrow may better remain unspoken, and what in the beginning appears the proper way of action, later can do more
evil than good.

Precisely on the fast-developing social stage of the United
States, Merton had found how so-called consistency and logic
often lead to despairing absurdity. The temptation to hold fast
to a once-chosen technique or form of action is all too great.
Who can recognize the moment that the old solution becomes
senseless? Not those who have buried themselves in strategies
and techniques, nor those who expect good to come from a
method, whether this is now called nonviolence or revolution.
If one does that, then one will go on with actions that have

become absurd, just because they seemed fruitful once long ago (see *Conjectures*, 156).

These reflections forced Merton to go deeper than the level on which contradictions exist. He had seen that what is called good luck by one becomes bad luck for the other, what is called justice here is called injustice there, and what is sought by virtue and merit slips away at the moment people think they possess it. This experience forced him to ask: "Am I concerned then with conquering happiness, peace, and justice? Am I concerned with joy, love, patience, and the rest as objects of my striving?" Chuang Tzu made him alert for these questions. Merton wrote:

> Chuang Tzu . . . believes that the whole concept of "happiness" and "unhappiness" is ambiguous from the start, since it is situated in the world of objects. This is no less true of more refined concepts like virtue, justice, and so on. In fact, it is especially true of "good and evil," or "right and wrong." From the moment they are treated as "objects to be attained," these values lead to delusion and alienation. Therefore Chuang Tzu agrees with the paradox of Lao Tzu, "When all the world recognizes good as good, it becomes evil," because it becomes something that one does not have which one must constantly be pursuing until, in effect, it becomes unattainable.
>
> (*Way*, 22–23)

Merton noted that Chuang Tzu, who seldom worked with reasoning but spoke in pictures, said:

> When the shoe fits
> The foot is forgotten,
> When the belt fits
> The belly is forgotten,
> When the heart is right
> "For" and "against" are forgotten.
>
> (*Way*, 112)

Merton is accused by many critics of being against technology and not valuing the great conquests of objective science. Especially after the publication of *Conjectures of a Guilty Bystander*, some were disappointed by Merton's relativizing of the great discoveries of modern humanity. His statements come, however, out of a very different source than one might think. He is not the monk who looks down with contempt on the busy, complicated, technical world and lives rather in virgin nature. He is instead one who asks himself whether what we win with the right hand is not lost by the left. Merton had studied not only Chuang Tzu but also Claude Levi-Strauss, the anthropologist and founder of structuralism.

His ideas of the Western technological culture had also sparked Merton's interest in the question of whether the modern means by which we try to reach our ends really lead to human advancement. This question preoccupied him until his death. In his diary he wrote: "Today with a myriad of instruments we can explore things we never imagined. But we can no longer see directly what is right in front of us" (*Conjectures*, 281).

The core of this problem lies in the Western tendency toward objectivizing and externalizing. Is it perhaps that the most valuable things we want to gain with technology are already present within ourselves? Chuang Tzu expressed this in his own poetical manner:

> If a man steps on a stranger's foot
> In the marketplace,
> He makes a polite apology
> And offers an explanation
> ("This place is so terribly Crowded!").

> If an elder brother
> Steps on his younger brother's foot,
> He says, "Sorry!"
> And that is that.

> If a parent
> Treads on his child's foot,
> Nothing is said at all.

> The greatest politeness
> Is free of all formality.

Perfect conduct
Is free of concern.
Perfect wisdom is unplanned.
Perfect love
Is without demonstrations.
Perfect sincerity offers
No guarantee.

(*Way*, 138)

The thought that what is most holy permits no blind externalization or objectification gave Merton even more concern, since his life was a search for God. He wrote:

The more one seeks "the good" outside oneself as something to be acquired, the more one is faced with the necessity of discussing, studying, understanding, analyzing the nature of the good. The more, therefore, one becomes involved in abstractions and in the confusion of divergent opinions. The more "the good" is objectively analyzed, the more it is treated as something to be attained by special virtuous techniques, the less real it becomes. As it becomes less real, it recedes further into the distance of abstraction, futurity, unattainability. The more, therefore, one concentrates on the means to be used to attain it. And as the end becomes more remote and more difficult, the means become more elaborate and complex, until finally the mere study of the means

becomes so demanding that all one's effort must be con-
centrated on this, and the end is forgotten.... This is,
in fact, nothing but organized despair: "The good" that
is preached and exacted by the moralist thus finally becomes evil, and all the more so since the hopeless pursuit
of it distracts one from the real good which one already
possesses and which one now despises or ignores.

(*Way*, 23)

All people who study theology must feel themselves chal-
lenged by these words. The questions are unavoidable: Does
all our talk and discussion about the divine bring us closer to
God? Does our intelligent analysis and our detailed working
out of the mystery of salvation bring us closer to the source
of truth? Does the constantly greater emphasis on theology as
an objective science open the way to the One we seek? Or
is it true, as Chuang Tzu said, that we have become blind to
the One we already possess, and that we try desperately with
ever more complicated means to get a hold on the God we
seek, but who continually remains beyond our grasp?

Merton said that this manner of relating to God was organized despair, which makes good into evil, God into Satan. Are
we the kind of theologians who can be happy only when God
is a problem? Chuang Tzu said:

If an expert does not have some problem to vex him,
    he is unhappy!

If a philosopher's teaching is never attacked,
 he pines away!
If critics have no one on whom to exercise their spite,
 they are unhappy.
All such men are prisoners in the world of objects.

(Way, 141)

Non-action

Is there no way out of this impasse? If there were no exit, then Merton would have become bitter and given up upon noticing that a certain planned strategy had no results. He had already heard from Gandhi that nonviolence was more than a tactic, a strategy, or a technique, and demanded a nonviolent heart that could be formed only in solitude by prayer and fasting. Chuang Tzu, who lived more than two thousand years before Gandhi, helped Merton further on this path. He led him from nonviolence to non-action.

And it is just this non-action from Chuang Tzu that Merton saw as a way out of our estrangement from God. He wrote:

"My greatest happiness consists precisely in doing nothing whatever that is calculated to obtain happiness.... Perfect joy is to be without joy.... If you ask 'what ought to be done' and 'what ought not to be done' on earth to produce happiness, I answer that these questions do not

have [a fixed and predetermined] answer" to suit every
case. If one is in harmony with Tao — the cosmic Tao,
"Great Tao" — the answer will make itself clear when the
time comes to act, for then one will act not according
to the human and self-conscious mode of deliberation,
but according to the divine and spontaneous mode of
wu wei, which is the mode of action of Tao itself, and is
therefore the source of all good. (*Way*, 24)

For Merton this meant: The closer God is, the less means
are necessary. Even words become superfluous in speaking
with God. The one who has no more words has found God.
Chuang Tzu said:

> The purpose of a fish trap is to catch fish, and when the
> fish are caught, the trap is forgotten.
>   The purpose of a rabbit snare is to catch rabbits.
> When the rabbits are caught, the snare is forgotten.
>   The purpose of words is to convey ideas. When the
> ideas are grasped, the words are forgotten.
>   Where can I find a man who has forgotten words? He
> is the one I would like to talk to. (*Way*, 154)

This non-action also holds for the contemplative life itself.
It is striking to see how, toward the end of his life, Merton
relativized the contemplation about which he had written so

many books, booklets, articles, and pamphlets. In a lecture he gave in October 1967, he said:

> I would say that it is very important in the contemplative life not to over-emphasize the contemplation. If we're always thinking about contemplation, contemplation, contemplation, union with God, mystical union, and intimate experiences with God, etc., that's fine, that's all very well. But if we constantly over-emphasize those things to which access is inevitably something quite rare, we overlook the ordinary authentic real experiences of everyday life as real things to enjoy, things to be happy about, things to praise God for. (*Contemplation*, 351)

Perhaps Merton had experienced even more the artificiality of the distinction between contemplation and action. Chuang Tzu had showed him this sharply. Merton wrote:

> A contemplative and interior life which would simply make the subject more aware of himself and permit him to become obsessed with his own interior progress would, for Chuang Tzu, be no less an illusion than the active life of the "benevolent" man who would try by his own efforts to impose his idea of the good on those who might oppose this idea — and thus in his eyes, become "enemies of the good." The true tranquility sought by the

"man of Tao" *is Ying ning,* tranquility in the action of non-action, in other words, a tranquility which transcends the division between activity and contemplation by entering into union with the nameless and invisible Tao. (*Way,* 26)

Chuang Tzu said this as follows:

> Fishes are born in water
> Man is born in Tao.
> If fishes, born in water,
> Seek the deep shadow
> of pond and pool,
> All their needs
> Are satisfied.
>
> If man, born in Tao,
> Sinks into the deep shadow
> Of non-action
> To forget aggression and concern,
> He lacks nothing
> His life is secure.
>
> Moral: "All the fish needs
> Is to get lost in water.
> All man needs is to get lost
> In Tao." (*Way,* 65)

Seen in this way, non-action means not only avoiding goal-oriented plans and strategies in order to find happiness "somewhere outside," but also avoiding introverted self-analysis. Non-action (which does not stand in contrast to activism) is a consequence of the experience that God is not an object that can be conquered as a possession, but is the all, in which we can lose ourselves.

And in this experience, all the old has become new, without essentially changing, since the contradiction between old and new had also fallen away. From this comes the Zen saying:

> Before I grasped Zen, the mountains were nothing but mountains and the rivers nothing but rivers. When I got into Zen, the mountains were no longer mountains and the rivers no longer rivers. But when I understood Zen, the mountains were only mountains and the rivers only rivers. (*Zen*, 140)

There still remains the question: What can the East teach the West? The answer from the East is once again: nothing. The East can only awaken what has fallen asleep in the Western consciousness. Chuang Tzu said nothing that had not already been heard by Merton within the Christian tradition. Nevertheless Buddhism kept him intensely preoccupied, especially after the meeting with Suzuki. This meeting made a deep impression on Merton:

In meeting him one seemed to meet that "True Man of No Title" that Chuang Tzu and the Zen Masters speak of.... In meeting Dr. Suzuki and drinking a cup of tea with him I felt I had met this one man. It was like finally arriving at one's own home. (*Zen*, 61)

Merton, who had already studied Buddhism and was often confused by the many mysterious words, images, legends, and rites, was freed from this by Suzuki.

Kenosis

The most important of Merton's studies of Zen Buddhism are *Mystics and Zen Masters* and *Zen and the Birds of Appetite*. The first is composed especially of descriptive studies, in which Merton tries to give as clear a picture as possible of what Zen Buddhism is, and the second directs itself especially to the dialogue with Christianity. It is appropriate that we end our study with a few remarks on *Zen and the Birds of Appetite*, published in 1968, in order to better appreciate the last phase of Merton's life and thought, which led him to Bangkok, where he died.

When Merton asked himself where precisely the East can open the eyes of the West, he returned continually to the meaning of *kenosis*, the self-emptying that holds such a great place in both the Eastern and the Western mystical traditions, but that in the West, unfortunately, is largely lost through the dubious glorification of the "ego."

The feeling of self-importance of activity-oriented Westerners depends greatly upon the question of what they can achieve, or what power and influence they have. They judge others according to what they possess, how much they produce, how much money they earn, and how many contacts they have. Such persons have put the *self* in the center of their thought. For the Westerner, Merton said:

> The concept of the self as a clearly present, very concrete center of decision has considerable importance. [For people preoccupied by the self,] it matters very much what you are thinking, saying, doing, deciding, here and now. It matters very much what your current commitments are, whom you are with, whom you are against, where you claim to be going, what button you wear, whom you vote for — all this is important. This is obviously proper to men of action who feel that there are old structures to be torn down and new ones to be built. But from such men we must not yet expect either patience with or understanding of mysticism. (*Zen*, 29)

We modern Westerners are so busy with ourselves, so preoccupied with the question of whether we do justice to our own selves, that the experience of the "transcendent" becomes practically impossible. In the way of thinking that involves talking, discussing, analyzing, and criticizing, in which one opinion asks the other for attention, in which belief is replaced more and more by an endless list of conceptions, opinions, visions, and ideas that whirl around as paper boats on the sea — in this way of thinking there is scarcely room for the God who speaks whenever we are silent and who comes in whenever we have emptied ourselves. Instead of making ourselves susceptible to the experience of the transcendent God, we, busy with many things, begin to seek after the small flighty sensations brought about by artificial stimulation of the senses. Merton recognized the danger of glorifying the ego even within the contemplative life itself. He noted:

> It becomes overwhelmingly important for us to become detached from our everyday conception of ourselves as potential subjects for special and unique experience, or as candidates for realization, attainment, and fulfillment. ... This means that a spiritual guide worth his salt *will* conduct a ruthless campaign against all forms of delusion arising out of spiritual ambition and self-complacency which aim to establish the ego in spiritual glory. That is why a St. John of the Cross is so hostile to visions, ecstasies, and all forms of "special experience." That is why the Zen Masters say: "If you meet the Buddha, kill him."
>
> (Zen, 76–77)

Merton hopes that perhaps the East could help us again recognize the Christian sense of *kenosis,* self-emptying. The actual experience of God will never really be possible if we are constantly busy with the cultivation of our own personalities by a spurious spirituality. The Zen Buddhist can point out to the Christian the possibility of self-emptying and searching for a direct and pure experience of the transcendent, freed from all self-preoccupation. To the extent that we deemphasize our "self," the need to understand God in verbal formulas and linguistic constructions also disappears.

Merton hoped that whenever Christians have the courage to renounce this concern with self, they would also find the actual meaning of the Christian experience of God:

All transcendent experience is for the Christian a participation in "the mind of Christ" — "Let this mind be in you which was also in Christ Jesus . . . who *emptied* himself . . . obedient unto death. . . . Therefore God raised him and conferred upon him a name above all names" (Phil 2:5–10). This dynamic of emptying and of transcendence accurately defines the transformation of the Christian consciousness in Christ. It is a kenotic transformation, an emptying of all the contents of the ego-consciousness to become a void in which the light of God or the glory of God, the full radiation of the infinite reality of His Being and Love are manifested. (*Zen,* 75)

Just as the black person must bring the white person to conversion, so must the East make the West Christian again. With this conviction Merton went to the East. On December 10, 1968, in Bangkok, a few hours after his lecture on Marxism and the monastic ideal, he met death by electrocution when he came into contact with a faulty electric fan.

The U.S. Army officials in Bangkok provided the embalming and coffin and flew his body in a U.S. Army plane back to Kentucky. Seeing the irony of this, former abbot Dom James Fox remarked: "True enough, I'll wager he had a good laugh in Heaven at all this" (Letter by Dom James Fox about Merton's death, 5).

FOR MEDITATION

On Chuang Tzu's value for Christianity

I simply like Chuang Tzu because he is what he is and I feel no need to justify this liking to myself or to anyone else. He is far too great to need any apologies from me. If St. Augustine could read Plotinus, if St. Thomas could read Aristotle and Averroes (both of them certainly a long way further from Christianity than Chuang Tzu ever was), and if Teilhard de Chardin could make copious use of Marx and Engels in his synthesis, I think I may be pardoned for consorting with a

Chinese recluse who shares the climate and peace of my own kind of solitude, and who is my own kind of person.

(*Way*, 9–11)

On what is truly good

The more one seeks "the good" outside oneself as something to be acquired, the more one is faced with the necessity of discussing, studying, understanding, analyzing the nature of the good. The more, therefore, one becomes involved in abstractions and in the confusion of divergent opinions. The more "the good" is objectively analyzed, the more it is treated as something to be attained by special virtuous techniques, the less real it becomes.... This is, in fact, nothing but organized despair: "the good" that is preached and exacted by the moralist thus finally becomes an evil, and all the more so since the hopeless pursuit of it distracts one from the real good which one already possesses and which one now despises or ignores. (*Way*, 23)

On happiness

"My greatest happiness consists precisely in doing nothing whatever that is calculated to obtain happiness.... Perfect joy is to be without joy ... if you ask 'what ought to be done' and 'what ought not to be done' on earth to produce happiness, I answer that these questions do not have [a fixed and predetermined] answer" to suit every case. If one is in harmony with Tao — the cosmic Tao, "Great Tao" — the answer will make itself clear when the time comes to act. (*Way*, 24)

On the absolute

[For Zen,] The Absolute is in no way distinct from the world of discrimination.... The Absolute is in the world of opposites and not apart from it. (*Zen*, 3–4)

On the aim of Zen

The chief characteristic of Zen is that it rejects all these systematic elaborations in order to get back, as far as possible, to the pure unarticulated and unexplained ground of direct experience. The direct experience of what? Life itself. What it means that I exist, that I live: who is this "I" that exists and lives? What is the difference between an authentic and an illusory awareness of the self that exists and lives? What are and are not the basic facts of existence? ...

The whole aim of Zen is not to make foolproof statements about experience, but to come to direct grips with reality without the mediation of logical verbalizing. (*Zen*, 37–38)

On Christians and Zen

Is it therefore possible to say that both Christians and Buddhists can equally well practice Zen? Yes, if by Zen we mean precisely the quest for direct and pure experience on a metaphysical level, liberated from verbal formulas and linguistic preconceptions. On the theological level the question becomes more complex. (*Zen*, 44)

On the message of Zen

Now in Zen, what is communicated is not a message.... It is not a "what." It does not bring "news" which the receiver did not already have, about something the one informed did not yet know. (*Zen*, 47)

"Zen teaches nothing; it merely enables us to wake up and become aware. It does not teach, it points" (Suzuki, *Introduction*, 38). The acts and gestures of a Zen Master are no more "statements" than is the ringing of an alarm clock.

(*Zen*, 49–50)

Merton's Prayer

My Lord God, I have no idea where I am going, I do not see the road ahead of me, I cannot know for certain where it will end. Nor do I really know myself, and the fact that I think I am following your will does not mean that I am actually doing so. But I believe that the desire to please you does in fact please you. And I hope I have that desire in all that I am doing. I hope that I will never do anything apart from that desire. And I know that if I do this you will lead me by the right road, though I may know nothing about it. Therefore I will trust you always though I may seem to be lost and in the shadow of death. I will not fear, for you are ever with me, and you will never leave me to face my perils alone. (*Thoughts*, 81)

Acknowledgments

Crossroad extends special gratitude to the Henri Nouwen Centre (www.HenriNouwen.org), Sue Mosteller, and Maureen Wright for their initial permission to reprint this volume and later assistance in the preparation of this volume.

For works by Thomas Merton:

Seeds of Destruction and *Thoughts in Solitude*. Reprinted by permission of Farrar, Straus and Giroux, LLC: Excerpts from *Seeds of Destruction*. Copyright © 1964 by The Abbey of Gethsemani. Copyright renewal 1992 by Robert Giroux, James Laughlin, and Tommy O'Callaghan. Excerpts from *Thoughts in Solitude*. Copyright © 1958 by the Abbey of Our Lady of Gethsemani. Copyright renewed 1986 by the Trustees of The Thomas Merton Legacy Trust. *Faith and Violence* — permission granted by The Merton Legacy Trust. Excerpts from *My Argument with the Gestapo* — copyright © 1969 by The Abbey of Gethsemani, Inc. Used by permission of Doubleday, a division of Random House, Inc. Excerpts from *The Sign of Jonas,* copyright © 1953 by The Abbey of Our Lady of

Gethsemani and renewed 1981 by the Trustees of The Merton Legacy Trust, reprinted by permission of Harcourt, Inc. Excerpts from *Gandhi on Non-Violence* (edited by Thomas Merton), copyright © 1964, 1965 by New Directions Publishing Corp. Reprinted by permission of New Directions Publishing Corp. Excerpts from *The Way of Chuang-Tzu*, copyright © 1965 by The Abbey of Gethsemani. Reprinted by permission of New Directions Publishing Corp. Excerpts from *Zen and the Birds of Appetite*, copyright © 1968 by The Abbey of Gethsemani, Inc. Reprinted by permission of New Directions Publishing Corp. Most of the Merton selections derived from the volume originally known as *The Secular Journal* now appear in a posthumous collection of Merton's journal writing, *Run to the Mountain: The Journals of Thomas Merton, Volume One 1939–1941*. Selections from this book (by Thomas Merton and edited by Patrick Hart) appear copyright © 1995 by The Merton Legacy Trust. Reprinted by permission of HarperCollins Publishers Inc. Rights to the small number of selections not appearing in *Run to the Mountain* are currently held by The Merton Legacy Trust (*The Secular Journal:* permission granted by the Merton Legacy Trust). Crossroad extends gratitude to the Merton Legacy Trust for permission to reprint these selections. Excerpts from *Conjectures of a Guilty Bystander* (Doubleday, 1968; 1989) — copyright © 1966 by The Abbey of Gethsemani Inc. Used by permission of Doubleday, a division of Random House, Inc.

Index of Names

Nouwen Book Ideas
for Every Reader

People reading Henri Nouwen for the first time will enjoy *Life of the Beloved: Spiritual Living in a Secular World.* Written as a direct and personal note from Nouwen to a friend with no training in theology or religious thought, this book, with a reflection guide, has become a classic in classrooms and seminaries.

Business, church, and adult education leaders turn to *In the Name of Jesus: Reflections on Christian Leadership* for insight. This book, which helps us understand the special nature of being a leader following Jesus, is widely assigned in seminary and adult education courses and parish training. It includes a study guide.

For daily reflection, turn to *Here and Now: Living in the Spirit.* Use this book for bedside and pocketbook reading, or use it, with the major reflection guide, as the basis for a weekly prayer meeting.

For Lent, keep a copy of *Show Me the Way: Daily Lenten Readings.* Each day includes a scripture verse, reflection, and prayer.

To delve more deeply into Nouwen's thought, especially on the intersection of spirituality and our worldly lives, read Nouwen's challenging *Finding My Way Home: Pathways to Life and the Spirit* (now in paperback, with a reflection guide), and learn about Nouwen's approach to questions of peace, power, and waiting. Then read *Encounters with Merton* to see how the young Henri Nouwen understood the insights of another great spiritual teacher. Finally, *Beyond the Mirror: Reflections on Death and Life* is a short book examining Nouwen's near-death experience and the meaning of life.

True Nouwen fans will appreciate *Sabbatical Journey: The Diary of His Final Year.* This was Nouwen's final book, written in the last year of his life, and is a treasure of intimate details of Nouwen's life and thought.

Crossroad also offers two excellent anthologies of Nouwen's work, prepared by people who knew Nouwen and are committed to preserving his message. Wendy Wilson Greer offers us *The Only Necessary Thing: Living a Prayerful Life,* the finest and most lovingly assembled treasury of Nouwen's work ever prepared. And in *The Heart of Henri Nouwen: His Words of Blessing,* Rebecca Laird and Michael J. Christensen take four key themes Nouwen announces in *Life of the Beloved* and show how they help us understand Nouwen, both as a writer and as a man beloved by those fortunate enough to have known him personally.

Please support your local bookstore,
or call 1-800-707-0670 for Customer Service.

For a free catalog, write us at

THE CROSSROAD PUBLISHING COMPANY
16 Penn Plaza, 481 Eighth Avenue
New York, NY 10001

Visit our website at
www.crossroadpublishing.com
All prices subject to change.

People interested in learning more about Henri Nouwen's legacy, ordering books, and signing up for free inspirational messages are invited to visit the Nouwen Centre website at *www.HenriNouwen.org.*